I0796037

What Others Are Saying

As an editor and writing coach for the past 40 some years, ***Out of Balance Into Rhythm*** has been by far the most inspiring and delightful work I have had the privilege to edit. I will go so far as to say I believe this book is a culture changer for the church, the body of Christ. Frank Maycock is a sincere, humble, inspiring man of God who finds joy in sharing Him with others and seeing the Lord work in their lives. Read this work with an open heart and mind, and you will never be the same. Editing it has impacted me profoundly; studying it has changed my life!

—SUE SHELLEY
EDITOR

As a non-believer who wishes to understand the Christian perspective for his own edification, I found ***Out of Balance Into Rhythm*** to be an extraordinary read. Dr. Maycock takes an approach that I find both unique and admirable. With decades of experience as a minister in addition to his Doctor of Ministry degree, he offers interesting and compelling viewpoints from which all readers can benefit. Dr. Maycock provides not only his thoughts on living in the rhythm of Christ, he provides life lessons. Whether you embrace the Christian faith, follow non-Christian beliefs, or are a non-believer like me, ***Out of Balance Into Rhythm*** can help you come to a better understanding of yourself and others.

—JOHN ELLIS
EDITOR

We have had the privilege of reading ***Out of Balance Into Rhythm*** prior to publication. The author's emphasis on God's rhythm has had a major impact on our lives. After years of using the word "balance," we realize now that what we truly meant was rhythm. Frank Maycock's book is a timely reminder that living in God's rhythm is tantamount to living in His abounding grace moment by moment. We highly recommend this book.

—JACOB & IRENE COVER
FERROSAFE, LLC

The author relates so well to the situation that many believers find themselves in: having salvation, but missing joy, contentment, abundance, peace, and power. He describes with clarity and precision how and why we end up in this discount version of a new life. From this clear vantage point, Frank begins to paint a picture of God's deep desire for us to experience life with Him, in the fullness of goodness. The rhythm of God drawing us into this experience, this "new creation" life He paid so dearly for, is then revealed, and we see His way of leading us "from glory to glory," going deeper into relationship with Him in each cycle.

This message has life-giving and world-changing power, and it comes not as an academic or theoretical or idealized expression in Frank's writing, but as a reflection of his own journey with our Lord. I believe other readers will clearly recognize the message as God's revelation to them through one man's very real journey. I cannot adequately describe the difference his discipleship has made in me, a believer for 24 years. Through these truths, God has given me a compelling gospel that I love to share.

—**Mike Bauman**

Business Owner, Selah WA

Dr. Frank Maycock has an open and refreshing way of explaining how God works in our lives, and his choice of Bible passages to support his writing is brilliant. Dr. Maycock is a theologian, but his words combined with the Scriptures are not at all preachy or haughty. As he writes, you see that he is walking on a similar path facing the same ordinary struggles. In the end, this book will fill you with hopefulness and a determination to move closer to God in your daily life.

—**Carolyn Ross**

Administrative Assistant & Coaching Client, Chicago IL

For several decades, I have shared the journey of life with Frank Maycock. Throughout our time together, he has always had a desire for a deeper and closer relationship with the Lord. It took a rather catastrophic event in our lives to make us realize that our relationship with the Lord should be more about being with Him, not just doing for Him. The words in this book tell the good news that God loves each and every one of us and desires to be in relationship with us. Each day I see how these words are reflected in Frank's life and that has helped me draw closer to the Lord myself.

—**Cindy Maycock**

Wife, Mother & Teacher

Frank Maycock

OUT OF BALANCE INTO RHYTHM

Finding Joy & Peace as You Live Life with God

Parsons Publishing House
Christiansburg, Virginia USA

Out of Balance Into Rhythm
by Frank Maycock

Parsons Publishing House
Christiansburg VA 24073 USA
www.ParsonsPublishingHouse.com
Info@ParsonsPublishingHouse.com

ISBN -13: 978-1-60273-078-6
ISBN -10: 160273-078-4
Library of Congress Control Number: 2016903278
Printed in the United States of America.
For World-Wide Distribution.

Acknowledgments

Simply writing a page like this puts me at a place of humility. Years ago I was told, "There are no original thoughts." I agree with that, especially when it comes to theological and biblical matters. From the beginning of time, God set in place His Word and His Spirit to allow us, His creation, to partake in what it really means to reach our fullest potential as humans. Consequently, I believe that somewhere, someone else is thinking and feeling what I have for quite a long time; I simply have the honor of putting it down in writing. I am not an island; I have had the privilege of being exposed to some of the great theological constructs, great minds, and wonderful people who were willing to listen to my thoughts and feelings. What you have in this book is the chronicle of a journey that has created a change in me as I have been assisted by many other people who impacted me along the way. For those with whom I have had the pleasure of dialoging and pontificating some of my thoughts, I express my deepest gratitude.

For the professors throughout my life who have challenged me to think differently, and for those who encouraged me to not simply know the material, but to persevere and apply it to my life, I thank you. For those professors who gave me the privilege of one-on–one time, whether in the car driving from the hotel to classes, taking me to lunch, sharing your thoughts and feelings with me, or the times in your offices when I felt welcomed and valued, I thank you as well.

I remember the joy I had in seminary with two friends, Kevin and Ray, who allowed me to sit with them and simply talk through theology. I remember the long trips I had with Rob, riding from California to the state of Washington, talking through some of the thoughts of people we either had heard in person or read. To me these are rich experiences that have helped me grow.

For the several pastors in my life who truly reached out and not only told me about Jesus, but showed Him to me, I am indebted to you as a lamb that is thankful for his shepherd's protection and watchful eye. The list could go on from church to church as well, remembering the hundreds of sermons people were willing to listen to as I studied and tried to give the gospel message the best way I knew how at that time. For your love, support, and grace during those times I thank you.

To one of my editors and friend, Sue, this book would not have been written if it were not for your friendship, support, and encouragement. There were many times when I got stuck and you simply said to me, "Just write! Even if it is 'blah, blah, blah' hundreds of times, just write, and inspiration will come." Those words of encouragement and support I hope will not go unrewarded as I have had the privilege of accomplishing through this book thoughts and feelings bottled up for years and only allowed few people to hear them. For your husband, Joe, for allowing you the time to help me with the writing and editing of this book, I thank you. I also want to thank the other members of my mastermind team who have supported and encouraged me.

To my darling wife, Cindy, my two wonderful children, and my daughter-in-law, you have shown me more grace, mercy, love, and support than any person deserves, I thank you. I am a blessed man having the four of you by my side helping me in times and ways that have spurred me on to be a better man and a more gracious father. You are the recipients of many of my shortcomings and I hope as time goes on I can give to you all the love and support you deserve.

Finally, I thank the Lord Jesus Christ; this book would not even be possible if it were not for Your grace, love, and sanctifying work in my life. I cannot properly express how much I love You. You have given me a rhythm to live by and a way to see You that helps me, and now I get to share it with others. For this, I thank You and want You to know how blessed I am for You coming into my life and being with me through my ups and downs and through my struggles and victories. You have never left me, nor forsaken me. In the dark moments I have come to realize You were there all the time; I simply did not recognize it. You also helped me to realize that I am enough, and with Your help I have the privilege of spreading Your Word by sharing that revelation with others.

Table of Contents

"There is a time for everything, and a season for every activity under the heavens" (Ecclesiastes 3:1).

SEASON III – From Comfort to Discomfort

SEASON IV – From Independence to Dependence

Foreword

Who or what gets the best of you? This is a question I first began to ponder when it was posed in a sermon by a dear friend of mine. It's a question I find myself trying to answer on a continual basis. I've tried to answer it many times in my life, in my ministry, and in my preaching.

It is a question that drives me loopy when I'm brave enough to answer honestly. Perhaps you can relate with that crazy feeling as you spin your wheels trying to juggle and balance all of the areas in your life where you are striving for success.

Put that thought aside for a moment because you are holding in your hands one of the rarest of books. I've read hundreds—perhaps thousands—of books about life, faith, spirituality, and Jesus. My personal interest fuels this passion, and my profession as a pastor demands it. Throughout all of this reading, I've been told what to do, what to think, what to read, what to say, and even what to feel. In these books, I've been pushed to do something different.

Out of Balance Into Rhythm is not a book that forces you to do anything. It is a rare book in that the words that flow from the ensuing pages will not push you, but rather usher and lead you. You'll be invited into a journey and a process instead of being shoved into hurried action. Let's face it, most of us have plenty of harried action already.

Frank Maycock has been used by God in a powerful way in my life and in our church body. I believe that you will find that he has been used by God in this book to bless you with the words, thoughts, and heart to not push you, but to LEAD you away from the abrupt and superficial work of doing things and into a new rhythm of being the person God created you to be.

When you consider the question of who or what gets the best of you, I can imagine that like many people, your head is filled with competing options that all battle for your best effort…but what if effort isn't the end goal of faith? What if accomplishment isn't the quantification of discipleship?

As you are led on a journey through the following pages, I invite you to allow God to speak words of value, hope, love, and identity directly to your heart. I dare you to open yourself to a God who loves you in a progressively knowing way that will finally answer the question you've been asking.

As you consider who or what gets the best of you, you'll find that the journey the author is about to lead you on will unfurl the lavish love of God in your life.

It's time to stop juggling and balancing. May the pages that follow help you uncover your rhythm with a loving God.

Your fellow journeyer,

Sam Middlebrook
Lead Pastor, Christ the King Community Church
Yakima, Washington

Introduction

For years I have heard the phrases, "You need to live a balanced life" or "All I need to do is find the balance." I have to admit that the concept of balance is intriguing because it begs the questions:

- "What does balance look like?"
- "How do I know that I am living a balanced life?"
- "Is balance different for me than what it is for someone else?"
- "What happens when a couple thinks they are living a balanced life, but it is actually sending them in opposite directions from each other?"
- "Has anyone ever truly lived a balanced life?"
- "Is living a balanced life even biblical?"

I could go on, for questions run through my mind like water coming out of a faucet in full force.

What I think people are saying is that there is something innate going on inside their beingness that feels out of sync. So we have coined the phrase "out of balance" as a way to describe that feeling. The problem is that when we hear the word "balance" we tend to go into a linear mindset that causes us to think about what balance might look like. Then we begin to adjust our thinking, wondering if we really want to live differently.

For example, a businessman grabs a cup of coffee, kisses his children good-morning, says good-bye to his wife, then jets out the door at 7:00am for an hour commute to work. Once he is at work, he is so focused on what he is doing that before he realizes it, it is 4:00pm and he still has several things to get done before he can leave the office. So he cracks down and gets his work done, leaves the office at 7:00pm and makes the hour drive home. He comes in, kisses his wife, and is just in time to tuck the children into bed and say good-night. He then sits down to eat a reheated dinner and looks at the mail. He may spend an hour relaxing before drifting off to bed only to begin over again the next day. This routine is part of his life until the weekend, when he fills his days with paperwork that did not get done, mowing the yard, attending his children's sporting events, watching football on TV for a while and maybe, just maybe, he interacts with his wife and others. He attends church and feels good for another week and then starts all over again. This person might say he needs more balance, but what does that really look like?

Balance is one of those aloof words we use to justify change, but then we change and go back. We return because it is not balance that we seek, it is something else we long for but cannot identify. It is something that our spirits or hearts, minds, bodies, and souls seek; it is that very thing that we hunger and thirst for and every once in while we catch it, feel it, sense it, and do not take the time to find out what it is. So we call it balance in hopes of positioning our lives in such a way that we find peace. We strive to live our lives the way we balance our checkbooks—making sure our accounts are reconciled to the penny. Can we live our lives like we balance our checkbooks? Some people try, then wake up in their 50s or 60s thinking they have done everything right, but are lonely and dissatisfied because they have never truly lived. They have simply attempted to stay in balance, doing everything right just like the Good Book says.

The terms *rat race, chaotic lifestyle, driven*, and others are used to describe a life that we believe is out of balance. We live this way because we either do not know better or we just want to fit in. Values and principles are done away with as we strive for success and the appearance of happiness. The world keeps moving us further and further away from the very thing that God created us to be. We are driven by the mantra, "I want what I want, when I want it, the way I want it." Balance then becomes anything we make it out to be, and we find ourselves rationalizing our lives seeking the things of the world versus the things of God; we seek what makes us happy for the moment rather than what sustains us for a lifetime and beyond. We seek opportunities that look good, smell good, and feel good at the time only to seek something else later on as those things we have invested in wash away like soil on a hill as the rain continuously pours down. To keep us from eroding too fast, we use the word *balance* to shore up the soil in hopes that we will not slide down the hill of life with nothing to show for our time on this earth.

We also have adapted terminology as a means of seeking the elusive balance, in hopes of setting the stage for the performance we choose to live out every day of our lives. Words such as love, stewardship, commitment, integrity, service, and mission are used. These are words that have punch and meaning, and imply to others that we are in the know, not simply drifting along without a destiny or purpose. So we work like animals, live nicely, become slaves to our lifestyles, and then go on a vacation or a mission trip once a year and call that balance. Financially, we give a specific amount to certain causes, no more or less, and we call that stewardship and perfect balance. The story about the poor widow who gave all she had becomes something we cannot attain because we live a "balanced life."

What is the recipe for a balanced lifestyle? I would be intrigued to have someone show me in the Bible where anyone who committed all they had to Christ lived a balanced life. I know there are many books that address it, but how can you be balanced? We are great at shifting priorities, adding or taking a little away from our lifestyles, but is that what the Lord requires?

Admittedly, I do not have all the answers to these questions but I do, however, have a conviction and passion that tells me that living a balanced life does not work for me if it gets me into doing and not being. We are human beings, not human doings.

For me there is an alternative, and it is found in the word "rhythm." This book will begin to explore what rhythm looks like in one's life and how it calls us to a place of being and not doing, because the doing comes in that moment of our beingness. If we change the rhythm, we can change the way we think, feel, act, and respond to the world's call for balance. Rhythm puts us in a place where we can be self-differentiated, as Edwin Friedman describes in his books, ***Generation to Generation*** and ***A Failure of Nerve***. A self-differentiated person is one who does not let the world around him affect his beingness. He creates a space for others to stand in their beingness and allows change to occur for himself as he chooses, while not allowing his life to be altered as a result of the emotional situation or circumstances he is experiencing at that moment.

With my premise I admit that I may offend some religious orders, eschatological traditions, every humanistic tendency, and many thoughts that we believe come from God. Stated simply, each of these events, feelings, situations, struggles, challenges, joys, and expressions of faith are simply in and out of the rhythm that God has put into place. The more I try to make something happen, or try to make something look a certain way, the more I stand in jeopardy of presupposing I know everything I need to know and experience about God.

Don't get me wrong, I am a staunch evangelical who sees, believes, and knows what it means to be a Christo-exclusivist. It is only Christ and the work of the Holy Spirit in my life that allows me to write these thoughts and feelings, knowing they will be read by believers and skeptics alike. These thoughts and feelings have always existed in some form, and we, in Christ, have the key to the future, the key to the questions, and thus the key to the answers of how to live in God's rhythm.

Many people have said to me, whether in person or in a book that history repeats itself. We can rationalize that phrase, dissect it, and diagnose it all we want. We can even ignore it, but no matter what we do with that phrase, it is a part of the past. What hasn't been determined or understood by man is what will happen in the future. No matter how we strive to change the future or interpret the past, no matter how we put our best foot forward, we will not know the outcome of what we are doing today as it impacts the future until the future comes. Francis Schaeffer titled one of his books with this question, ***How Should We Then Live?*** My contention is that we live in the present with all the fullness, understanding, and feelings we have in the moment in hopes that what we say and how we live will have an impact on what happens tomorrow.

Out of Balance Into Rhythm expounds upon the idea that if we walk in the rhythm of God as He created us and live according to His Word, we can better understand how our decisions affect our present and future. This rhythm can be seen as a series of seasons helping us to understand the ebb and flow of life and where God is in the midst of those seasons. Within each of these seasons we find God has placed stepping stones to help us become more grounded and have a solid place to cling to until we move into the next season with Him. It is in understanding these seasons and seeing the stones in place that help us make a positive difference in our own lives and in the lives of others, celebrating His glory until the Lord reveals Himself in the flesh and shows us the fullness of a life that is totally and passionately devoted to Him.

Season 1

From Isolation

To Relationship

Chapter 1
From Chaos to Order

"And God said, 'Let there be light,' and there was light" (Genesis 1:3).

Years ago I coined a phrase for myself. When people ask me who I am, I sometimes respond that I am a person who believes in planned spontaneity. I love to know what is going to happen next. I do not like to live in the unknown or make choices based on the unknown. I have been part of a leadership development program where people frequently ask, "Are you up for a challenge?" Upon hearing that question, my heart cringes and my immediate response is, "No," because I do not know what they are going to ask, nor do I know the outcome.

I understand that my concerns here stem from a lack of trust, but that question puts my mind into a state of confusion because I am not comfortable with it. I want to know what is expected of me and what the expected outcome is. Once I have collected sufficient data, I will then give my answer.

Like many others, I approach life from an analytical point of view. I can think of more questions in a ten-minute period than most people think of throughout their day. I sometimes envy the person who can just say, "Yes," and not worry about what that challenge might look like, feel like, or be concerned with what will happen after the fact.

When I find myself on this analytical side of life, it affords me the opportunity to look at things differently from how others might. One such area is in the creation story found in the book of Genesis chapter 1:1-2 which reads, "In the beginning God created the heavens and the earth. Now the earth was formless and empty, darkness was over the surface of the deep, and the Spirit of God was hovering over the waters."

This has been one of the most debated verses in the Bible. It speaks of creation versus evolution, the plan of God, God's existence, His involvement in the world, and the list goes on. What has intrigued my mind for years is the phrase: "The earth was formless and empty." As I have read and studied these verses, and read other people's opinions, what fits my line of thinking and my heart as a believer is first of all the Trinity—Father, Son, and Holy Spirit—three persons, yet one God, existed before the creation of time, space, and life as we know it today. Secondly, and just as vital in this passage, is the reality that nothing existed but God, and creation occurred when God spoke it into being. That thought alone sends shivers up my spine when I think about the power of His Word, the power of His shaping and forming life simply by speaking everything into existence.

His Word, both written and spoken, has the ability to change the world as we know and experience it, and changes the thought that things should happen a certain way. He speaks; life happens and the world comes into existence. There is something so sweet, so powerful about that phrase, "And God said..." God created something out of nothing; God takes chaos and creates order. God takes a formless substance and turns it into something precious; He creates life. Now we can get into a debate as to what that might look like, but that is not my purpose here. For me the focus is life. It is the start of something that was not and now exists. It is something that only He could imagine into existence and beingness to become a reality. Out of something that was chaotic, He created a system or order that speaks of rhythm and seasons; something that breathes and has its very being come into form and substance simply because God said.

It is in this sweet and powerful story that we discover a God who can make something out of the chaos of life and turn it into something of beauty. He is a God that speaks life and it happens. What was not now is because what God says, He does. Some people may say that is a utopian feeling without substance, fact, or reality. To those people I would encourage you to look at the rhythm of God to see, feel, and experience that everything you are going through has purpose and meaning. If you are willing to see Him in these chaotic, disturbing, disruptive moments in creation and in your life, He will show you His glory, splendor, and love. It comes not because we ask for it, but it is only in the asking that we may be open to see it. God's voice, His presence, is always here; it was in the beginning of time when there was nothing and it is here today. Before time came into reality the Holy God was hovering over the earth.

Following are some examples from my own life that I hope will lead you to understand the rhythm God has created and how He can bring His order out of the chaos in each of our lives.

One day, as I was driving toward the church where I served at the time and felt the urge to stop by the house of a woman who had just lost her husband. I was taken aback by what she said as she opened the door. "How did you know? I was praying and getting ready to call you." God said...

When I was nine years old, I was listening to someone preach. I don't even remember what he said or how he said it, but I went forward. I was taken into the corner of the room and asked to pray to receive Christ as my Lord and Savior. I prayed and immediately began crying tears of joy. What happened and how did it happen? God said...

I have seen couples who were told they could never have a baby so they adopted, only to get pregnant. How? Why? God said...

I have seen people survive car crashes that should have killed them, but they walked away. How? Why? God said...

My friend once experienced a man with a gun held to his head. When the trigger was pulled, the gun jammed, and his life was preserved. How? Why? How was God speaking in this circumstance?

Conversely, I have known situations in which a couple prayed to have a baby and never could conceive, people who are prayed for to receive salvation and they die before accepting Christ, people who have died in car crashes. I have seen a mother and father leave one morning and come home to find their daughter shot to death. How was God speaking in these circumstances?

God is sovereignly in control, and He is speaking in times of blessings and of tragedies. God's sovereignty means He has supreme authority. It does not mean that He picks and chooses who will respond to His gift of salvation. It does mean that God is present and will speak to our hearts and minds in each of those situations. He can lead us to see that something horrific, tragic, and totally incomprehensible from a human perspective still reflects His glory as He turns it into something of power and beauty.

This is something mysterious that our minds cannot fully grasp because it comes out of a rhythm that God put into place at the beginning of time. This rhythm showed up when He took something that was formless and void and turned it into something beautiful and marvelous simply because God said…

God is still speaking to us in our lives, in the victories and in the voids. As we experience life, chaos, disappointment, or tragedy, we can find God's rhythm when we learn to hear what He is saying at all times.

Chapter 2

The Start of Something Big

"My command is this: Love each other as I have loved you. Greater love has no one than this: to lay down one's life for one's friends. You are my friends if you do what I command" (John 15:12-14).

In chapter 19 of the book of Luke there is a plea from the teachers of the early Jewish faith known as Pharisees. They were asking Jesus to rebuke the crowd because they were heralding Him as King. Jesus' response to them was simply, "'I tell you,' he replied, 'if they keep quiet, the stones will cry out.'" For some this may be a confusing thought. The reality is that Jesus wants people to see that He is the King of Kings and Lord of Lords, and He is also referencing that the heart of creation is to glorify the Lord in the fullest.

What does this really mean to us? When God created the heavens and the earth He could have stopped there. Creation itself was enough to signify His power, His glory, and to lift Him up. Everything in creation cries out praise to Him. He did not need to create man; He chose to create him. The Lord of the heavens and the earth chooses to be in relationship with each of us. The Bible goes on to say, "Then God said, 'Let us make mankind in our image, in our likeness, so that they may rule over the fish in the sea and the birds in the sky, over the livestock and all the wild animals, and over all the creatures that move along the ground'" (Genesis 1:26). It was God's choice to create, to separate, to coordinate, and to subjugate all of creation. Creation has an order to it, it has seasons, and it functions in a rhythmic fashion that God has orchestrated from the beginning of time.

Just look at a very familiar passage written by King Solomon in Ecclesiastes 3:1, "There is a time for everything, and a season for every activity under the heavens." That purpose was and is orchestrated by God Himself. Creation has no power apart from the power that God allows. To say differently would be to say that the world was formed another way and that the rhythm of life can be altered. It would be saying that we can alter the existence of the rhythm of life that has been created by God. Due to mankind's choices, confusion is created that interrupts the rhythm and order of things. But the rhythm as to how things operate remains constant according to God's plan.

I am not a scientist; I am simply a man who has accepted by faith and logic that there is an order and that order has been created by something other than us. Based on Scripture, that creator is God, and He loves to be in relationship with us. This relationship is more than we ever can see completely without the eyes of the Holy Spirit revealing it to us in our thoughts and hearts.

Let's go back to Genesis 1:26, "Then God said, 'Let us make mankind in our image, in our likeness." There is a vital pronoun in this passage that is oftentimes ignored by readers. That pronoun is "us." Some religious orders see the "us" as many, that there is more than one god. If this were the case, we would have to deal with the great Shema prayer in Deuteronomy 6:4, "Hear, O Israel: The Lord our God, the Lord is one." This opens more questions around creation which may be rationalized, or we can come to the understanding that God has a purpose, reason, and rationale for all things, which is consistent with who He is. Then we can accept who He is or create our own faith and justification for why we believe what we believe.

The consistency of Scripture from Genesis to Revelation supports the understanding that there is one God who has chosen to manifest Himself in three different persons known to us as Father, Son, and Holy Spirit. The book of Genesis supports that understanding in the pronoun "us." What God is saying is from the beginning of time there has existed all three persons in the oneness of God. This is known as the doctrine of the Trinity.

In that moment of creation, the Holy Spirit was a reality, and He continues to manifest God's splendor and glory throughout history and in our lives today. This revelation is what we can draw on each day as we seek and strive to understand the relationship that God has for each of us. That relationship takes a personal response from us. We have a choice to accept the relationship as God intended it to be with Him or to try and figure out a way to create a relationship based on my own thoughts and feelings. I want a relationship with Him, and when I have it the way He created it to be there exists a rhythm that goes beyond time, reason, and rationale. It is a relationship built on love, and the outgrowth of that love on my part is respect and choice.

I contend that the problem we have in life is that we continue to strive to create God in our own image. We want God to perform for us, when we want, the way we want, and how we want it, and when He doesn't perform, we question His existence or justify ourselves with a rationale for living life our way. We play a game in life that some call "blame, shame, and guilt." It is a game that does not serve anyone and only creates more problems. Consciously or unconsciously, we invite God into that game and create a "theology," or more appropriately, an "ideology" that fits our way of thinking and feeling. Then we can become confused and wonder why our lives and the world are in a chaotic mess.

The rhythm that God created in life is very simple: *I am God and you are mankind.* That being said, the Lord has created a way of life that, if we are willing to follow it, will lead us to the greatest relationship known to mankind. God is not as interested in how we are justifying our lifestyle as He is in the relationship He has designed and created for us to have with Him. It is a relationship built on trust, honor, and respect for all mankind as He designed. In this relationship with Him, we can live a life pleasing and honoring to Him.

Chapter 3

The Power of Love

"And now these three remain: faith, hope and love. But the greatest of these is love" (1 Corinthians 13:13).

You will never find a better definition of love than in 1 Corinthians 13. Paul lifts up love and shows us the purest form of the most powerful gift known to mankind. We cannot manufacture it or create it; it is simply there for the receiving. We long for it, we find ways to attach ourselves to it, we try to live it, and we strive for it without realizing that all we need to do is receive what has already been given to us. When we open our hearts and receive it, it will flow out of us powerfully, easily, and naturally.

This love is a statement of fact, not something we can strive to obtain. It is there at all times and in all circumstances. It is not something that needs to be worked on or a construct that we need to develop, it is there for us in every situation or conflict. It existed before the beginning of time and it will last throughout eternity. The love that I am referring to is God's love. It is a love that knows no bounds, that transcends time and space, and is often misunderstood and misinterpreted.

Due to the complexity and overwhelming power of His love, either we live in the midst of it and never notice it, or we touch the edge of it like the bleeding woman in Mark 5 and are healed and transformed as a result of it. This is a love that moves mountains and has driven people to sacrifice everything that this world holds of value. In order for us to grasp this gift let's examine some stories in Scripture that demonstrate different components of this fabulous love.

Redemptive Love

Redemption is a word not used much today unless you are in Christian circles. My mind goes back to a time in my childhood when pop bottles were worth two to five cents apiece. I would go around the neighborhood looking for bottles so I could redeem them by reclaiming their value and use that money to buy candy at the local drug store. Redemption is reclaiming the value of something that may be seen by others as broken, worthless, or damaged.

We see a great picture of a redemptive love in the story of creation. In Genesis 2 the Lord God gave a very specific command. Adam and Eve could eat of any tree in the garden with the exception of the Tree of Knowledge of Good and Evil. If they ate of it, the Lord said, "You will certainly die." In Genesis 3 we read that they ate of the tree and then heard God walking in the garden. In verses 8 and 9 we read, "Then the man and his wife heard the sound of the Lord God as he was walking in the garden in the cool of the day, and they hid from the Lord God among the trees of the garden. But the Lord God called to the man, 'Where are you?'" The Scripture clearly points out that Adam and Eve knew they were in the wrong. Out of fear and shame they hid from the Lord God. They did not go after Him with hearts of confession; instead He came running after them. He then dressed them with the skin of an animal. This was the first sacrifice the Lord made on our behalf. They defied His Word, and God reclaimed them. Did their actions cost them? Yes, they did, but the redemption of the relationship was evidence that God was reclaiming them.

There is a similar story in the New Testament in Luke chapter 15 in which the youngest son, a prodigal, returns to ask forgiveness of his father with the hope that he could at least be a servant to him. We read in verse 20,

"So he got up and went to his father. But while he was still a long way off, his father saw him and was filled with compassion for him; he ran to his son, threw his arms around him and kissed him." In the Jewish culture fathers did not run like that, but the father was so pleased at seeing his son that he ran and reclaimed him. He slaughtered an animal and held a giant banquet, for his son was lost but now he was found.

In both stories the common theme is God's redeeming love for us. He loves us so much that He goes out of His way to reclaim us. We see this love time and again throughout Scripture. This is the story of the cross, the all-inclusive act. The sacrificial Lamb of God comes from heaven to earth to reclaim all of humankind. There is a great hymn penned by Charles Wesley that captures this amazing love as we sing, "Amazing love how can it be that Thou, my God, shouldst die for me?" Jesus Himself died to reclaim us, to redeem us so we can be the sons and daughters of the Father. We did nothing to earn it; it is a gift that allows the God of creation to look upon us as His children. He is showing us a picture of what it means to be a true father, our *Abba,* which in the Aramaic language means "Daddy."

Redemptive love is a love that is evident in the worst possible situations. Yet that is the love that God gives freely, and it continues to be given throughout all time.

Correcting Love

There are two main lenses through which we can understand discipline. The first is **punitive**, which is the understanding of discipline simply for the sake of discipline. This is the mindset of a person or group driven by their own personal agenda and passions. Whether it is in prejudice, rage, anger, vindictiveness, repulse, or what have you, the punishment is harsh. It can be direct, and over obsessive to those who are watching, or to the recipient. The second is **corrective**, which is a correction of the behavior so that it does not happen again. It's about finding a way to discipline actions with an outcome that encourages those corrected to engage in more effective and healthier behaviors. It is discipline driven by selfless love.

Many people look at the Old Testament and read stories like the flood, or God's desire to wipe out an entire nation due to their behavior, and see God more punitive than corrective. If that is the mindset, the next question that usually arises is, "How is that loving?" When I parented my children and I had their best interest in my mind and heart, I found that the discipline came from a place of love, love that would bond us closer than their current behavior would. When I was focused more on me and how their behavior needed to change because it would either look better for me (like when we were in public) or would make me feel better at the time, that discipline was more punitive in nature.

When we look at Scripture and the acts of God through the eyes of love, we see that everything God did He did because He loves us. This reality serves us as finite creatures who are limited to human knowledge and lack the ability to comprehend infinity. We do not know all things past, present, and future, and should not try to look at God through our finite lenses. God Himself is infinite, and is the same yesterday, today, and forever. He is consistent and He knows all things, and everything He does is for the purpose of drawing us to Him. He realizes how much we need Him and how we are blessed when we see things through the eyes of love, even when it comes to discipline. So when God is concerned, all discipline is corrective and moves us as a society, a nation, and world to have a greater understanding of how we should live, see, and experience the benefits of living that kind of lifestyle.

Let's take the flood as an example and let me illustrate how this was an act of love and not punitive discipline. In Genesis 6:11-12 we read, "Now the earth was corrupt in God's sight and was full of violence. God saw how corrupt the earth had become, for all the people on earth had corrupted their ways." In these two verses we discover the nature of mankind; all flesh had corrupted their way on the earth. The Lord shows us a culture that is driven by that corrupt nature; our thoughts and ways do not follow after God innately (Isaiah 55:8) and only His Word can discern our motives (Hebrews 4:12). We also find in this same story how corrective love grows out of redemptive love. In Genesis 6:8 we read, "But Noah found favor in the eyes of the Lord." What we clearly read is that God pursues redemption, but it means He goes through the gateway of correction to show us His love. As we look at the flood we see that although many people perished, Noah and his family were redeemed because of their beliefs.

I do not pretend to fully understand why God does what He does, or why He allows what He allows. What is really happening when a catastrophe results in the death and suffering of seemingly innocent people, young and old alike? It happens because we live in a corrupt world and the Lord allows actions to occur to the just and unjust in accordance with the His order of life. God has built within His creation a rhythm of restoration, or cleaning. Fires occur naturally to allow the forests to grow. Our bodies reject poisons so we strive toward healthiness. Within creation there is a rhythm and God takes chaos and turns it into something that heals and benefits generations to come. If we try to correct chaos apart from love, we create greater chaos and then we see a world living in greater confusion and independence from God.

God uses both the divine means (i.e. the flood) and the natural course of events and uses it to correct what is going awry. It may not look the way we want, or how we think it ought to look, but we are not God and are therefore incapable of understanding His plan. When we try to play God we find ourselves creating chaotic reactions and results.

For some this creates a great crisis of faith. What should one do, for example, when faced with cancer or some other life-threatening illness? To know the answer to this question, we must open our hearts and see that first of all God has purposes for a greater good which we may not be able to understand at this moment in time. At the same time we must recognize there may be something going on in our choices that have perpetuated an illness or a problem. To narrow it simply to one answer is like trying to be God in that moment, where if we allow ourselves to embrace God and not be God, we can experience the fullness of Him in love no matter what we are facing.

I am not an ethicist trying to solve the world's problems; I am merely presenting a lens that may help us make wiser choices for ourselves and others. Through this lens, we find the hand and heart of God each and every day. When we open our hearts to Him we can see that things happen for a reason—whether natural or divine—that may be beyond our intellectual grasp. I am not infinite, but He is and He comes to us with a heart of love for all people in every situation, whether we see it or not at the time. This corrective love is simply a love that leads us to obedience, because it is a love that calls us to be our best.

Empowering Love

The more we accept and allow correction from God, the more we can see how His love empowers us to acts greater than we can comprehend. Read the story of Moses and you begin to realize just how powerful we can be. One day, while he was in the land of Midian and tending his father-in-law's sheep in the wilderness, Moses saw a bush at a distance that was on fire but not being consumed. As he approached the fire he was told to take off his shoes as the land he was standing on was holy ground. It was there in that desert that his entire life changed, and he began to feel and see the empowering love of *Yahweh*. He spent 40 years dealing with God's correction for taking matters into his own hands back in Egypt; it was his zeal and misunderstanding of his power that caused him to spend 40 years in the wilderness. Then at God's chosen moment, he saw an unconsumed bush on fire and felt God's power. This was an empowering love. In Exodus 3, verses 7-10 it says,

> The LORD said, "I have indeed seen the misery of my people in Egypt. I have heard them crying out because of their slave drivers, and I am concerned about their suffering. So I have come down to rescue them from the hand of the Egyptians and to bring them up out of that land into a good and spacious land, a land flowing with milk and honey—the home of the Canaanites, Hittites, Amorites, Perizzites, Hivites and Jebusites. And now the cry of the Israelites has reached me, and I have seen the way the Egyptians are oppressing them. So now, go. I am sending you to Pharaoh to bring my people the Israelites out of Egypt.

It is in this account that we see an 80-year-old man by the name of Moses have his life turned upside down by empowering love. He was being asked to lead more than three million people through the desert to a land that was occupied by people who did not honor or worship the name of *Yahweh*. The Lord was asking Moses to take this people, who were slaves, away from their homeland and lead them to a land that was promised to Abraham, their forefather.

Discipline can either create bitterness in us or it can be the very tool the Lord uses to empower us to do His will His way and for His reasons. He was not asking Moses to do this alone. That is not how the Lord operates. In verse 12 of that same chapter we read, "And God said, 'I will be with you. And this will be the sign to you that it is I who have sent you: When you have brought the people out of Egypt, you will worship God on this mountain.'"

By today's standards, and based on what we think about retirement, call, purpose and wanting what I want, when I want, the way I want it, Moses could have simply stayed in Midian and taken care of his family, living comfortably until he died. But Moses knew deep inside that there was more to be had in his life. He had not lived out his greatness, so his beingness was yearning for something. It wasn't until that day that he stepped into the power that was always there. Did God just show up at that moment? Why then? It was God's timing, and perhaps Moses' heart needed to change. Some of the questions are not intended to be answered; simply, the lesson in Moses' story is to be followed.

Moses was empowered by the love of God to serve the greater good of the nation. Did this mean that everything went well from that moment on? No!!! Does this mean that Moses was never disciplined again because He got it right from that moment on? No! What it does mean is that the Lord God has a plan and purpose for each of us. We are never too old or too young to know what that is; it is to serve Him, to love Him, to honor and worship the God of creation. When we are willing to be open and serve Him no matter what, He will tell us and will be with us with that empowering love to walk us through each step. This empowering love is not a love that should be ignored or manipulated for our good, but is a love that is to be embraced, accepted, and responded to in like acts toward others. When we are willing, we will rock the world and find a rhythm in life unlike we have ever experienced before. With Him we can move mountains, move millions of people from one place to another, heal the sick, and raise the dead; the list goes on as we embrace the fullness of His empowering love for us and for all mankind.

Transformative Love

When empowering love is felt and given away, we experience a transformative love; a love that transforms our hearts, minds, and lives of others. In Romans 12:1-2 we read:

> Therefore, I urge you, brothers and sisters, in view of God's mercy, to offer your bodies as a living sacrifice, holy and pleasing to God—this is your true and proper worship. Do not conform to the pattern of this world, but be transformed by the renewing of your mind. Then you will be able to test and approve what God's will is—His good, pleasing, and perfect will.

The man who wrote these words was a murderer—a man who lived in rage and anger against the people known as followers of Jesus Christ until the Lord met him on the road to Damascus. The story of Paul's conversion is found in Acts 9. It was on the road to Damascus that he was awakened by the Spirit of God and empowered in such a way that his life and the lives of generations have been transformed. In the words the Lord gave him and by his willingness to make a difference for the Lord, we discover transformative love. Paul not only wrote these words in the Scripture, he lived them, and he saw them accepted in the lives of others. So often I have heard people say they want God's will for their life or the life of their family and friends; if you want to know the will of God, then start living in accordance with these two verses.

God is about the work of transforming lives away from sin, shame, blame, and guilt. He is in the business of transforming lives. It costs us to sacrifice our way for God's way, our will for God's will, and our lives for the lives that God has designed for us from the beginning of time. Anything different may look good or feel good for a short time, but I guarantee you it falls out of the perfect, pleasing, and holy will of God. Until we die to ourselves, the Lord cannot transform us. Until we come to a place where we can live out the words that so many people say, "let not my will, but Your will be done," we will never come to that place where we can truly be transformed the way the Lord God desires.

Outside of the revealed Word of God, most of us are unaware of God's will at any moment in time. There are people who will give you dozens of answers on His purposes. There is much ignorance in our world under the umbrella of religion and spirituality. It takes discernment to understand God's rhythm in a situation. We are masters of dressing our words around logical doctrines that make sense. Our response may make us feel good and look good for that moment because we have done what we think the Lord has asked of us, but a week or month or years later we may come back to the same place if our minds were not transformed to the perfect, pleasing, and holy will of God. We may be convinced that what we were doing was the right thing because it made the most sense at the time; however, that is not always the case. Sometimes we are challenged only with good ideas, but we must hold out for the God ideas.

In Acts 16 we read how Paul and Silas were imprisoned for their faith. They had just been beaten, yet there they were in chains worshipping and praising God. In the midst of worship, the ground around them started to shake and lives were transformed as the jailer came to meet the Lord and step into His rhythm of life. Now that is transformative love. It came as Paul and Silas felt the redemptive, empowering, transformational love of God. When it comes you will find it is never about us, it is about Him for the sake of service and worship. When we are in that place in our love for Him we then see clearly the perfect, pleasing, and holy will of God.

Enduring Love

What is unfolding is a love that takes us deeper and deeper into a relationship unlike anything we can see or experience anywhere else in our lives. A love that once is captured can be the very love that causes us to endure the most difficult and powerful times in our lives.

In Acts 7 we read a story about a man who was called to be a deacon for the faith as he had the gifts of service; his call was to see that the widows and orphans were cared for. Within his ministry he was confronted by Jewish religious rulers who accused him of blaspheming the Lord. His response was to tell them about Jesus through the eyes of a Jewish believer quoting and defending His faith with the stories that each of these rulers knew better than anyone. As he preached, they became so angered at his words they stoned him to death. In this story we read,

> When the members of the Sanhedrin heard this, they were furious and gnashed their teeth at him. But Stephen, full of the Holy Spirit, looked up to heaven and saw the glory of God, and Jesus standing at the right hand of God. "Look," he said, "I see heaven open and the Son of Man standing at the right hand of God." At this they covered their ears and, yelling at the top of their voices, they all rushed at him, dragged him out of the city and began to stone him. Meanwhile, the witnesses laid their coats at the feet of a young man named Saul (Acts 7:54-58).

What would give a man such strength to endure the pain of the rocks on his body and feel the power and majesty of God? It was God's enduring love for him that empowered him to serve with such strength and commitment that it demonstrates a love that exceeds our normal understanding.

The other side of this enduring love is found in the Old Testament with the people of Israel on their journey to the Promised Land. Just after they were given the Ten Commandments and had consecrated Aaron and his family, Moses was talking to the Lord, and the Lord saw the people of Israel worshipping a golden calf. In Exodus 32 God turned to Moses:

> Then the LORD said to Moses, "Go down, because your people, whom you brought up out of Egypt, have become corrupt. They have been quick to turn away from what I

> commanded them and have made themselves an idol cast in the shape of a calf. They have bowed down to it and sacrificed to it and have said, 'These are your gods, Israel, who brought you up out of Egypt.' I have seen these people," the LORD said to Moses, "and they are a stiff-necked people. Now leave me alone so that my anger may burn against them and that I may destroy them. Then I will make you into a great nation" (Exodus 32:7-10).

The Lord wanted a people who really understood how much He loved them. The people of Israel were consumed only with themselves. No matter what He did for them, providing clothing, food, water, protection, and freedom, it wasn't enough to bring about the people's devotion, so He called them stiff-necked. It is in this journey that God's wrath showed its face for the disobedience of His people; He was ready to start over again. But His enduring love showed up with the words of Moses in verses 11-14,

> But Moses sought the favor of the Lord his God. "Lord," he said, "why should your anger burn against your people, whom you brought out of Egypt with great power and a mighty hand? Why should the Egyptians say, 'It was with evil intent that he brought them out, to kill them in the mountains and to wipe them off the face of the earth'? Turn from your fierce anger; relent and do not bring disaster on your people. Remember your servants Abraham, Isaac and Israel, to whom you swore by your own self: 'I will make your descendants as numerous as the stars in the sky and I will give your descendants all this land I promised them, and it will be their inheritance forever.'" Then the Lord relented and did not bring on his people the disaster he had threatened (Exodus 32:11-14).

Our actions toward God can continually sadden His heart, even to the point that He may want to start over knowing full well that His creation was already perfect. Unfortunately, creation is simply marred with sin as a result of allowing us to have the freedom of choice. The thing that we need to understand about His enduring love is that God chose to create us different from all other created things; He gave us that freedom of choice.

All other created things are driven by instinct. They were created simply to glorify the Lord in the way He designed them to worship Him. He gave us the freedom to choose and placed a tree in the garden at the beginning of creation so we could see the power of choice at work.

We were created perfectly, but His wrath demands obedience and His love offers grace. The tension of the two lives with us daily, and the evidence of that tension can be felt and seen in the enduring love of God. He continually allows His people to make choices even when we do not truly understand the rhythm of our relationship with a God who loves us with an ever-enduring love.

Responsive Love

Responsive love is like the most colorful, flawless diamond with the Lord Himself as the diamond cutter. He cuts the facets for us, showing the brilliancy of His love daily. All we have to do is look around with eyes open wide and simply see how much He longs to be in a covenantal relationship with us. This covenant that He established with Abraham and communicated down through the ages can be summed up in the words of Jeremiah 30:22, "So you will be my people, and I will be your God." This is a covenant that God has established and there is nothing we can do about changing or renegotiating because it is a unilateral covenant. It is a covenant that God created in His loving response to the world and all we can do is opt in or out.

He is God, *Yahweh*, Elohim, Jesus, The Great I Am, The Son of Man...No matter how He has described Himself in His Word, He is God and He has chosen to establish a covenantal relationship with us centered and driven through His love. This is God's response to us, what is our response to Him? Based on our response, we can see the rhythm that the Lord has created and wants us to live in. As long as we live within that rhythm, we can experience what Jesus prayed in Matthew 6:10, "Your kingdom come, your will be done. On earth as it is in heaven."

It doesn't come in a balanced life, but in a willingness to open our hearts and experience a love that nothing on earth can satisfy but God Himself, who responded to us in the person of Jesus. Jesus said it Himself in John chapter 15:

> Greater love has no one than this: to lay down one's life for one's friends. You are My friends if you do what I command. I no longer call you servants, because a servant does not know his master's business. Instead, I have called you friends, for everything that I learned from my Father I have made known to you (John 15:12-15).

Jesus bled the love of God in order for us to see and experience love unlike anything in this world. The more we embrace Him and His love and choose to enter into these expressions of God's love, the better we can begin to feel and experience His rhythm-His design-for our lives.

Chapter 4

Experiential Moments

"Taste and see that the LORD is good" (Psalm 34:8a).

Somewhere in my life I adopted the phrase, "This is a teachable moment." I have discovered that when I am conscious of this concept it helps keep my emotions in check, and I can see times of crisis or chaos as a gift. In that moment, I get to experience something as a blessing from Christ; I get to grow and learn about myself or others through a teachable frame of mind. In all reality, it seems like every moment has the potential to be a teachable moment. That can be true for all of us if we are willing to see life more as a journey than a series of goals. Too often I see people living each moment through the eyes of a goal. High schoolers can't wait until they get into college, college students can't wait until they are out of college and have a job, and working people can't wait until they retire. If we see life more as a journey than a destination, we experience a deeper and more personal relationship, first with God, then with ourselves and others. This is the experience that God created in the garden, to walk with Him daily with our hearts open to all He has for us each moment.

This answers some questions I have had as I walk this journey. How can two people go through the same events in life and have two totally different experiences? How can two lovers share a bed—one is fulfilled and the other is not? How can two children, raised by the same parents, have different understandings and emotional reactions to the same experiences? My conjecture is that one person is processing the experience through the eyes of data alone and simply seeing life as moving from one destination to the next, while the other sees through the eyes of the heart, embracing each moment. The one who is willing to experience with the heart can see each encounter as a teachable moment. This allows the person to determine the outcome, while the former interprets that same event through his own filters and thus does not experience the fullness he could have enjoyed.

We, as adults, do this all the time based on the data and the programs in which we have been raised. In college I took a class on rock climbing. As a child I climbed many things, rocks, mountains, roof tops and the like, so taking this class was both exciting and intriguing for me. I went into the class thinking it would be easy until I found myself twenty feet off the ground, held by a thin rope with nothing but air beneath me. I began to shake, my knees became weak, and I pictured myself falling off the rock because this thin rope was not enough to support me. I talked myself into being overly afraid. It was in that moment of fear that I had a choice to either get off this rock as quickly as possible, simply accomplishing the task and moving on, or to use it as a teachable moment, push through the fear, and discover things about myself that I would not experience in any other way. Once I arrived at the top, I was told that the rope could support thousands of pounds. I could have chosen to be angry that they didn't give me that information before I began to climb and decide to never climb again. Or I could use it as a teachable moment and trust that the people in charge really were looking out for my best interest. Because I was willing to see this as a teachable moment, I continued to climb for several years and even went on to teach others.

Many people do not understand what actually occurs when we face those teachable moments. In that moment we lose what most call our "sense of balance"—things aren't working the way we want them to. So we unconsciously or consciously strive to get things back into our perception of balance, which is another way of saying we are out of control and want to get back into control. We want things to look the way we want them to look. What really happens is we lose sight of our truest heart, a heart that beats to the rhythm of God. We have simply lost sight of living wholly with a trusting faith in God. Out of that trust and faith, even in a time of fear, we can enter into an experience with our hearts, thus creating a more powerful revelation of God than someone who seeks balance outside of God's plan. This keeps us in the rhythm of trust and faith throughout the tension of risk and comfort. It has been my experience that **"balance" keeps the scary parts of our life at bay and keeps us from experiencing the extraordinary moments of life.**

We do that with anything in our lives. As children we possess an innate feeling of invincibility. The environment around us either takes that feeling away or supports it. Kids are often influenced by superhero images, taking on the attributes of a superhero and entering into that moment as if they truly were. When a negative experience counteracts that assumption, a child is left with the realization, "I am not a superhero." The more that experience repeats itself, the more timid, reserved, and introverted a person may become.

Deep down that child within us wants to be a superhero. So as adults, if we can move out of balance into rhythm, we can move out of time and space from the "rational" side of life or be abandoned to the space and time God has intended. When this happens, the experience becomes more powerful, more meaningful, more passionate, or intense, and we regain the confidence that once said, "I am a superhero." This doesn't mean that I get to jump off buildings; it simply means I choose to enter into a rhythm of trust and faith in God.

For example, there are many people who want to learn how to ride a motorcycle, but don't because of the data and fear associated with it. Those who ride overcame that fear, never had it, or have embraced the fear as part of the experience. That motorcycle rider may have as much fear of intimacy as someone else who fears riding a motorcycle, and so will move from one relationship to another, never committing to any one person. The risk may appear to be different, but it is the data and our desire to stay in balance that keeps each of us paralyzed.

There is a cry in all of us for a sense of balance. We want to play life safe. We may accept or even welcome risk in some areas of our lives, but only where we have overcome fear. For instance, a rock climber may not have a fear of bungee jumping, yet could have a fear of spiders or confined spaces because of a negative experience in his childhood.

Our lifestyles are controlled by a combination of actions or reactions that were communicated or demonstrated to us during our formative years. Most of us were able to embrace the freedom of being a child. I once heard Dr. James Dobson explain that our values are established in the first seven years of our lives and from that time on we tend to live according to those values. As I consider this in the context of freedom, I often wonder how limited we are in our minds and our hearts, based on either the lack of good values or an abundance of overly strict values that were placed on us during that time. As adults, how many opportunities or experiences have been hindered based on those values, or lack of values? How does all of this play into our beingness today?

How does this play out spiritually? I remember a time while I was in Sunday school and we were talking about trust. To demonstrate, the teacher had us close our eyes and then fall backwards into the arms of a friend. The experiment worked well to demonstrate to us that the Lord has put everything into place in our lives to create trust. He told us in His Word, as illustrated in the references below:

- Do not be anxious (Philippians 4:6)
- Trust in Me (Proverbs 3:5)
- Have faith (Matthew 17:20)
- I will watch over you (Genesis 28:15)
- God has a plan (Jeremiah 29:11)
- All things work together for good (Romans 8:28)
- You have support in your fellow believers (Hebrews 10:24)
- Pray without ceasing (1 Thessalonians 5:17)
- I am always with you (Matthew 28:20)
- I will never leave you nor forsake you (Hebrews 13:5)

There are many more; the point is He has created as safe an environment as possible for us to trust Him in every aspect of our lives. If we get lost in the moment and don't worry about the outcome, we can abide in Him to the point that we can do things like walk on water, move mountains, heal people, and use our extraordinary gifts to be extraordinary people. The only limiting factors are the ones that go against His Word, which means that we have to deal with interpretation issues not based on the opinions of man, but on the voice and Word of God through the direction of the Holy Spirit.

One has to move out of balance, out of complacency, out of that urge to not rock the boat, or to have all things without conflict. One has to move into rhythm to feel and experience all that God has for us at any given moment. When that happens we begin to experience what it is like to live on earth as it is in heaven, where someone can give Elijah the last of her flour only to experience a pot that never runs out (1 Kings 17); where a prostitute can trust a bunch of strangers and help them escape only to become an ancestor to the King of Kings and Lord of Lords (Joshua 2, Hebrews 11).

Rhythm takes us out of the moment of fear in the circumstances and places us into the hands of God to reach the place where no man can conceive on His own apart from His dreams.

What are the elements that move us from a life of balance to living a life of rhythm?

Faith ~ Trust ~ Love ~ Hope

These are the keys that move us out of ordinary moments into extraordinary experiences. The more we trust in God and step out in faith, the more we feel love—the more we can hope for something powerful to happen. It is this movement that takes us out of our heads and into our hearts, out of our unhealthy fears and into the possibility that all things can work together for good. **The more we let go of fear, the more we are driven by passion.**

We see in Genesis that when Adam knew Eve, that intimate union brought forth a child. In the same manner, when we are passionately intimate with our heavenly Father, we bear the fruit of that union. Inside of both unions, we must abandon our self-interest for the joy of the other. As a spouse should find passionate freedom in the marriage bed, we must find passionate freedom in our relationship with God. This is the experience that Solomon writes about throughout the entire book of the Song of Songs. It is a love story that captures the love between a man and wife and God and man. Yes, God and mankind. This is the rhythm for loving and being loved by God; a rhythm that exists because God has our best interest in everything He does. When we have the same heart as one to a lover we will find that relationship blessed and fulfilled.

The outcome of any relationship will not be the same if fear is in the mix. Not the fear that speaks of the "awe" of God, but the fear that paralyzes us and keeps us from experiencing life as God designed it to be whether it is between man and a woman or mankind and God. When trust and faith are unleashed and the relationship is not shackled by fear, the couple may find a rhythm within their relationship unlike anything they had ever hoped. Our relationship with God should be like this; abandoning yourself to His rhythm in all areas will allow you to experience God in a fully satisfying dimension.

Chapter 5
Connecting Points

"Truly he is my rock and my salvation, he is my fortress, I will never be shaken" (Psalm 62:2).

In order to understand God's rhythm and grasp the fullness of what this really means, we must begin with some basic suppositions. It is important that we understand these suppositions as criteria that affect our perception of God's rhythm and acknowledge that we have the ability to alter our beliefs, which changes what our faith looks like. We can still be connected without them, but it will not be as deep as it could be if we accept these basic assumptions. My goal is not to debate or prove these criteria, but if we accept them based on the Word of God we can see what He has in store for us in our relationship with Him, with all the completeness and fullness that it entails.

Criterion 1: We do not have control of the relationship God has with us.

God is sovereign; however, for some people this is a debatable issue. For those of us who can embrace God's sovereignty, we come to a rich depth in the relationship that He has created for us. In His sovereign ability, we can rest assured that He seeks and wants a relationship with us, and we cannot control how He feels, how He shows it, or how He communicates it to us. He is God, Creator, and Lord who is sovereign and infinite in all wisdom and understanding; therefore, we cannot control the kind of relationship He wants to have with us.

Criterion 2: We are asked to surrender our will for His will.

The more we surrender our will for His will, the more understanding and awareness we gain of His desires for us. Part of the reason we do not understand God or what is going on around us is simply that we think we know what is best for us, and we are unwilling to surrender our will for His perfect, pleasing, holy, and acceptable will (Romans 12:2). If we can surrender our will for His, we can be open to see and enter into experiences in life that ultimately show us the fullness of heaven on earth—which is His prayer for His people (John 17).

Criterion 3: The fullness that God intends to have with us is meant to be a full body experience.

In the great Shema found in Deuteronomy 6:5 the charge is, "To love the Lord God with all our heart, soul, and strength." It is said by some theologians that the trichotomy of man is considered here as "strength" equates to the flesh or body. Jesus added the mind to this list in Luke 10:27 to help us understand the fullness of that prayer. When we withhold any part of us, we cannot see the fullness that God has intended for us to experience. If we can "seek first His kingdom and His righteousness" (Matthew 6:33) with our whole being, the gates of heaven are open to give us a world of wonder, amazement, glory, and blessings throughout our life on Earth. If we are not open to yield any part of our beingness, we will have a disillusioned and confused concept of His relationship with us and our relationship with Him.

Note what the Lord is saying to us. He implores us to love Him with 100 percent of our being. He does not say love Him with 75 percent of your heart and 100 percent of your mind, or love Him 100 percent in your heart, but let your body continue in sin. No, He says love Me with all you heart, soul, mind, and body. Based on our attitude and actions we can see evidence of how a person truly loves the Lord, and based on those actions, we can see how much they are truly adhering to the voice of God. How many of us are simply adding and subtracting from the Word as we see fit for a particular moment? Are we saying we love God, but fill our minds with pornography, or gossip, or slander? Do we say we love God but violate our bodies as God's holy temple? Do we truly love our neighbors as ourselves? Husbands, have you died for your wives like Christ laid down His life for the church? These things can become barometers, or at least an understanding about whether our words and actions are congruent with God's Word.

The Relationship God Wants

With these basic beliefs grafted into our minds, hearts, bodies, and souls, we can see that from the beginning of creation, there is a yearning to choose God's love and desire for us. That choice has been blocked and distorted by sin, but nevertheless there is something innate within us that must worship something. We oftentimes do not call it "god," but it feeds our desires, our passions, and the deep longing within us that hungers for something. Centuries ago, the noted mathematician Pascal described man's condition as such, "There is a God shaped vacuum in the heart of every man which cannot be filled by any created thing, but only by God, the Creator, made known through Jesus." We are just not sure what that might look or feel like, how to fully experience it, or what we need to do to fulfill that hunger.

In the Old Testament, the children of Israel were caught up in keeping the Law. At one point, God spoke a warning through the prophet Isaiah, "The Lord says: 'These people come near to me with their mouth and honor me with their lips, but their hearts are far from me. Their worship of me is based on merely human rules they have been taught'" (Isaiah 29:13). Since then we have all been on a similar journey, investing ourselves in the created things and divesting ourselves from the Creator. What I mean is we seek happiness, joy, contentment, peace, and love in our families, our jobs, our hobbies, and our interests. Turn on the television and watch any channel, and you will see people who are investing wholeheartedly in those things that fill their passion and interest, whether it is shopping or painting their bodies with the colors of their favorite team. The list is endless for the things that we long for simply to fulfill that which our soul, our beingness, craves. Accordingly, we tend to settle from time to time for the little "g" gods in our lives; it is there that we find a moment of pleasure, peace, and contentment. That is until the little "g," whatever it is, no longer satisfies that which can only be satisfied by God Himself. When this happens, we begin to realize that we have changed the original assumptions that alter our perception of God's rhythm. I suggest that we be careful and not try to find the fullness of life we are seeking by trying to satisfy what only God can satisfy.

It is those of us who can go beyond the little "g's" of the world and step into the revelation of what God has created for us who will find that which truly satisfies every longing, craving, or need. It is in that desire that we step into whatever assumptions we have set before us. Without desire, without passion, we would be dead. Even if you say to yourself, "I have no desire, I have no passion; all I want to do is sit here and do nothing," realize that those words bring to the forefront your truest passion for that particular time in your day or life.

Our choices are built around our passions, but they are also built around our assumptions. Those beliefs come to us through history, values, logic (based on what we know or think at the moment), and relationships past and present. Those core criteria create what can be seen as tinted glasses that cause us to see and feel a certain way about the data with which we have been presented. They affect the endless choices that are waiting for us to step into.

It is through the scope of desire and the lenses of assumptions that we create the path we take in a particular moment. The scope and lenses help shape the experience we are choosing to enter into at that time or phase in our life.

If our desire is God and our premise is to follow in His paths and His ways, we can see a direction, but the pathway may look different from what we think or feel it should depending upon how much we choose to be in control. We may not arrive and we may not experience all that the Lord has in mind for us. It all depends on our perspective and the lenses we use to help direct us along the way. The more we live in those basic suppositions, the deeper our relationship and experience will be with the Creator who longs to have that special, intimate, and fulfilling relationship with us. This was His original intention for all of us to experience, providing we are willing to accept God being God, and let Him choose the pathway we are supposed to take.

Each of us may experience this path and its outcome in different ways. Take the tragic tornadoes that occurred in Oklahoma in May of 2013. You could interview thousands and find similar thoughts and feelings of fear and hopelessness, but you would also find in some people feelings of peace, joy, love, contentment, and understanding because the scope and lens they are looking through is the love and trust they have in the Lord. How deep that relationship must be with Him! How much are we willing to surrender to Him in our entire beingness in times like this? It is in times of crisis and separation that we come to a place of questioning God. It is in those questions that we discover just how deep, special, and powerful our relationship is with the Lord.

John said it best in John 15:1-2, "I am the true vine and my Father is the gardener. He cuts off every branch in me that bears no fruit, while every branch that does bear fruit he prunes so that it will be even more fruitful." Part of that fruit is an awareness of the love and relationship we have with the Father. The greatest fruit we can have in life is the fruit of that relationship—that connection we have with the Creator Himself.

"Taste and see that the Lord is good; blessed is the one who takes refuge in him" (Psalm 34:8). This fruit is evident, not because it hangs from the tree, but because it comes when we surrender and come together completely in the sovereign Lord, surrendering our will for His and giving Him every aspect of our lives, body, heart, soul, and mind, to do as He wills, when He wills, and how He wills.

That fruit is the experience of intimacy unlike anything the world can offer. If you had a choice to be given a box of apples or an orchard full of apples, which would you choose? One is easy for the moment and the other takes work, but which is more profitable? Why do we settle for a box of apples when the Lord is giving us an orchard? Why are we settling for momentary pleasure, peace, or contentment, when we can come together with a little work (which is learning to die to our ways and accept His) and enjoy the garden of God?

Chapter 6
Stepping Stones

"The Lord makes firm the steps of the one who delights in him" (Psalm 37:23).

At one time I had a job pumping concrete. It was my responsibility to move the concrete from the truck into the pump through the hose to where it needed to be placed. Oftentimes I would go to a job site and discover it was one big muddy mess, and I had to string out enough hose to move the concrete to its destination. At the end of the day, I would clean the pump and the mud-covered hose. Then I would clean my shoes; what a mess. There were some jobs that had stepping stones or solid concrete already poured, which made moving the concrete and cleaning up much easier. Stepping stones make life a whole lot easier. Instead of getting stuck or bogged down, or simply moving the mud from one place to another, they provide a foundation that makes the process less onerous.

How many of us live our lives that way? We are moving mud around only to cause ourselves more work. How many of us get stuck or take forever to get where we want to go in life because we get bogged down? Wouldn't it be nice to have such a relationship with God that we can see stepping stones wherever we go, no matter what we are facing?

We have been talking about many of the stepping stones that the Lord has put in place. They come in His Word; they come in the stories of people who have walked before us; they come in our embracing faith, hope, love, trust, grace, mercy; and acts that help move our beingness toward oneness with God. If we step on them we find that perfect rhythm that God created at the beginning of time which allows us to reach a oneness with God like Jesus describes in John 14-17. He describes His relationship with His Father, with us, and the relationship that He longs for us to have when we let Him lead our lives.

The stepping stones help us in a way that we can embody the life of God and not simply bring Him along with us on our journey. Years ago there was a movement that used the acronym WWJD which stood for "What would Jesus do?" As I understand it, the intent was for us to be conscious that Christ is present, and if we ask ourselves what He would do, we might find ourselves conforming to His will. It's good that some are at least talking about God-whether it impacts their actions or not; then there are some who have truly learned what it means to allow their actions to be changed by dying to self and letting Christ live in and through them. They are the ones who ask themselves, "What would Jesus do through me?"

One in Christ

By dying and allowing Christ to live through us, we discover a relationship through which we learn that He and we are one, just as He and His Father are one. We then realize that He is not just a role model to emulate. In John 14 one of Jesus' disciples asks Him to show them the Father. Jesus said to Philip:

> Jesus answered: "Don't you know me, Philip, even after I have been among you such a long time? Anyone who has seen me has seen the Father. How can you say, 'Show us the Father?' Don't you believe that I am in the Father, and that the Father is in me? The words I say to you I do not speak on my own authority. Rather, it is the Father, living in me, who is doing his work. Believe me when I say that I am in the Father and the Father is in me; or at least believe on the evidence of the works themselves.

> Very truly I tell you, whoever believes in me will do the works I have been doing, and they will do even greater things than these, because I am going to the Father" (John 14:9-12).

In this passage we see the Oneness of God and a mystery at the same time. The oneness is because He is only one God. The unity is because this one God has manifested Himself in three persons: Father, Son, and Holy Spirit. We call this the Trinitarian relationship. It is in this mystery and relationship that Jesus is helping us see the oneness that He has with the Father, because He and the Father are one. Being fully human while on earth, He had the same freedoms as you and I; the freedom to either do the will of His Father or to do His own will. We read that throughout His ministry on the earth He chose to do the will of the Father. We hear this clearly in the garden prayer right before He died on our behalf, when He said, "Father, if you are willing, take this cup from me; yet not my will, but yours be done" (Luke 22:42).

Jesus lived to do the will of the Father. What He wanted Philip and us to see is that to look at Him, to listen to His words, and to understand His relationship with the Father was to see the Father and His love for us. Jesus is the cornerstone by which all other stones are aligned for all mankind to encounter, embrace, and surrender. When we do, then we can experience His promise to us in John 14:15-18:

> "If you love me, keep my commands. And I will ask the Father, and he will give you another advocate to help you and be with you forever—the Spirit of truth. The world cannot accept him, because it neither sees him nor knows him. But you know him, for he lives with you and will be in you. I will not leave you as orphans; I will come to you."

This is a oneness that can be felt, experienced, and that helps us see the stepping stones and walk on them daily as we surrender our lives for His, our ways for His ways, our thoughts for His thoughts, and our actions for His actions. The Apostle Paul said it best, "I have been crucified with Christ and I no longer live, but Christ lives in me. The life I now live in the body, I live by faith in the Son of God, who loved me and gave himself for me" (Galatians 2:20). The more we are in sync with the Spirit of God who dwells in our hearts, the more we see and experience and become one with Him as He desires to be with us.

People who simply emulate His teaching, His life, His love, and so forth, fall short of that oneness where Christ is willing to walk in us, talk for us, heal through us, and live in us. All we have to do is die to ourselves, surrender our ways to His, and embrace the fullness of who He is and what He wants to accomplish in and through us. When we do this, we will see the miracles of God manifest around us. We can live a life with Christ in which He completely dwells in us to give us that relationship that empowers us into a deeper understanding of God, and a rhythm with Him that cannot be duplicated or emulated by anything we strive to do on our own, no matter who we are or how much we think we know. What this kind of relationship does for us is more than we can imagine. It can only be experienced, and once experienced we are made believers. The relationship that Jesus had with the Father is what He wants us to have, and it comes out of a heart that loves Him completely.

The Duality of the Heart

There is a duality that appears in some churches when in one sermon it is preached to love the Lord your God with all your heart, soul, mind, and body. In another sermon it is preached not to follow your heart, for your heart is deceitful. This can often leave the listener confused, because the Scripture proclaims both truths.

There are situations in the Scripture that can give us this tension of duality. Remember the words of Jeremiah, "The heart is deceitful above all things and beyond cure. Who can understand it?" (Jeremiah 17:9). What Jeremiah was talking about is a heart centered in self—a heart that is driven by the eyes and desires of man. Struggle results from that duality when we are driven more by what man says, or what we want, than by what the Spirit of God says.

Jesus tells us to love the Lord our God with all our heart. That is the same heart; the difference is that it is focused on the passion and desire for God, not for man or the things that God created. The heart is deceitful, but when I love the Lord God with all my heart, the heart is not wicked and deceptive. Moving from head to heart needs to be the work of the Holy Spirit in our lives, even before we receive Him and accept Him. It is God paving the way through the works and means of life that helps us see how empty we are without Him. Our heart can either pull us toward Him or take us away from Him.

The mystery that we grapple with is not our deceptive heart, but our need to know everything before we step out in faith and follow our heart's tug toward Christ. We will never be persuaded by words that the Gospel is the answer if our heart is not open to the thought and construct of such a possibility; this openness comes from the work of the Holy Spirit. When we focus on ourselves we will always be deceived. When we focus on the Lord and how to have a more effective relationship with Him, our heart will lead us to the answer that is reinforced in the Word of God, and that is to receive Christ as Lord and Savior.

Thus we discover a stone that we can hold onto or embrace that reminds us that it doesn't matter what we do, or what we believe; God is pursuing a relationship with us. This is a foundational piece that allows us to experience the fullness of a God who longs to be with us and in us from now into eternity. This stone is not a sign to follow but rather a marker of remembrance that allows us to reflect on His fullness and His desire for us as we enter into His rhythm.

Season 2

From Ideology

To Theology

Chapter 7

The Ideological Endeavors of Man

"Fear God and keep his commandments, for this is the duty of all mankind. For God will bring every deed into judgment, including every hidden thing, whether it is good or evil" (Ecclesiastes 12:13b-14).

How many times do we look at people a certain way only to discover what we assumed about them was totally wrong? Dating and engagements are among those times we have the opportunity to really get to know a person and discover who they are, how they function or don't function, and in what they are interested or not interested. In some ways it is like a dance to the music of life; we live in that moment, learning to dance with our partner. When we believe this is the right person, we jump in and marry them. Later, we discover that we did not know our partner as well as we thought—for better or for worse. How many of us have based decisions like this on our ideas or our ideology about them? So often we make decisions based on passing thoughts and ideological assumptions rather than from experience when another way of living can have a more positive impact throughout our lives.

Why do we allow ourselves to assume that what we see in a person or their behavior might one day be different than we thought and hoped for based on our perception? I am not a psychologist, nor will I attempt to explore this from a deep psychological understanding; however, my simple understanding says our perceptions are formed through our own lenses.

When the lenses change or we take them off, we either see differently or more clearly.

My contention is that we tend to see God the same way. We are prone to look at our situation in life through our perceptions and view our theology accordingly. The suffix "ology" means the study of a thing. When we put that with other words like psychos, anthropo, and even Theos, we have the study of the mind, man, and God. Christians have battled over theological issues throughout the centuries which have cost innumerable lives, ruined untold relationships, and destroyed more countries than we care to count. We have arguments over theological stances from baptism to the deity of Christ. We have used the Bible to support slavery and the same Bible to call it an abomination against mankind. We have combined theological opinions with the understanding of psychology and philosophy since around the time of Alexander the Great, when Greece hellenized the world, arguing the Word of God with a philosophical and apologetic format to this day.

The fascinating thing about all of this is that we have used the same Scriptures to argue every side. To add to that, because of one interpretation of the Scripture over another, we discover that everyone feels they are right when it comes to knowing God's will for everyone's life, including their own. When we are not using the Scripture, we are using our minds and a common thought process to argue our state of rightness. Whether you are a theist, an atheist, or one of the billions of people arguing your own theological stance, you are probably arguing from a state of perceived accuracy, whether it is out of the Bible, the Koran, or someone's reasoning.

In the midst of this great dilemma, how do we come to know God and follow His rhythm for all of mankind? I believe it starts from our state of *being*. That is to say, to be at the place we need in order to understand the Word of the One who wants to communicate it to us. How does this look? It comes from having a relationship with Him which He created us to have. It comes in our willingness to listen to Him as He chooses to communicate.

It also takes the work of the third person of the Trinity, the Holy Spirit. We could not begin to grasp the fullness of God if it were not for the work of the Holy Spirit guiding our hearts and thoughts toward Him. If we solely rely on ourselves we are simply arguing from an ideological view of understanding God. It is God who tells us who we are, what we are, who He is, and how we are called to live. When we do it His way completely we find more fullness and blessings in life than we could ever imagine and hope.

We have the Scriptures to help guide our thoughts and to show us how to live in accordance with His will. But living and understanding the Lord is more than reading the Word. Take the passage in Psalm 119:11 which says, "I have hidden Your Word in my heart that I might not sin against you." These are more than just words and more than a command to understand the Word. It is a call to be open and responsive to His voice and His way at that moment. It is not to focus on what He said but on Him first and foremost. Does that mean that we throw out His word? By no means, it is His Word to us. But unless we are living in a true relationship with Him, we will interpret the Word to say what we want it to say.

God, who is infinite and sovereign, does not want us to simply understand His Word, but to understand Him. This means that when we invest in a relationship with Him His Word helps us work through that relationship, but we have to be careful that it doesn't keep us from it. We get exclusive insight into God through the Holy Spirit, and when we lack wisdom He is there to help us and guide us so we don't misunderstand Him and go astray in our own interpretations.

Let me explain what I mean. In Exodus 20:8 it is written, "Remember the Sabbath day by keeping it holy." If you were to read the ***Jewish Mishnah*** you would discover that there are pages and pages of interpretation as to what that should look like. But the Jewish traditional thought was challenged by Jesus one Sabbath while He was walking through a grain field and scooped up some grain with His hand. Immediately, the Jewish leaders chastised Him for working on the Sabbath. In Mark 2:27 Jesus says, "The Sabbath was made for man, not man for the Sabbath." How perplexing if you are used to living a certain way and suddenly that way is challenged? How wonderful God is in helping us understand Him if we are willing to listen to Him each and every day!

Jesus helped the teachers of the Law understand that they were more concerned with honoring a day than honoring the Lord. It was a day to set aside, honor Him, and rest. Does that mean we can't work? Does it mean that as long as we go to worship we can do whatever we want? Or is it really about what we can and cannot do? If we are not careful we can create an interpretation that leads to a doctrine about what we should do, how to do it, when to do it, and what it will look like throughout the process. Just speaking that way makes me tired. Imagine trying to live that way. That kind of life knows about God, without really knowing Him. At the very least, it's about how He wants us to live and not about having a deeper and more intimate relationship with Him.

Psalm 103:7 says, "He made known his ways to Moses, his deeds to the people of Israel." Though Moses wrote the Law, he also knew the ways of God, but the children of Israel knew only His acts. We need to be more like Moses and understand the ways of God—the movement—the rhythm of our Father. I sure don't want to be in the company of only knowing His mighty deeds—though we get to know them, teach them, and live them out through His Spirit helping us each step each day, but He desires our hearts to be in that deeper place that turns a "have to" into "a desire."

There is another passage I want to show you in this discussion of creating an understanding of God through our own ideological thoughts and feelings. Leviticus 15:19 says, "When a woman has her regular flow of blood, the impurity of her monthly period will last seven days, and anyone who touches her will be unclean till evening." Then, in Mark 5:25-34 we read about a woman with a flow of blood who was unclean for 12 years. Can you imagine? Everyone she touched or who touched her, according to the Law, was unclean until night fall. So she had to stay away from people, and she did until Jesus came into town:

> When she heard about Jesus, she came up behind him in the crowd and touched his cloak, because she thought, "If I just touch his clothes, I will be healed." Immediately her bleeding stopped and she felt in her body that she was freed from her suffering. At once Jesus realized that power had gone out from him. He turned around in the crowd and asked, "Who touched my clothes?" (Mark 5:27-30).

What is God saying in these passages? Each of us begins our journey by starting with this question and from there we get to experience and hear Him. What is He saying? There was a crowd around Jesus and there she was pushing through touching whomever she needed to touch simply to reach Jesus. It did not matter about the Levitical Law. What mattered was that she ran into Jesus and she was healed. It sounds weird that Jesus would honor a woman who broke the Law like that, or does it?

What this story shows us is that Jesus understands the Law and the reason; He placed the Law there in the first place. If our standing with God were based on obedience or lack of obedience to the Law, then no one would be in right standing with Him. I am not saying we can live without the Law, but to place it in the context that God Himself has placed it helps us see more clearly what living the Law looks like.

When we follow the Law, the way we interpret it, the way we think is the right way, the way it makes sense to us, then I believe we run into the same problems as the teachers of the Law. Interpretation after interpretation, we settle either on the opinions of man or on our own conclusions. Whether we are the most conservative theologically or the most liberal, we follow the road of ideological constructs, making it mean whatever we want. Throughout history we discover that this process is given credence when we get a group of people to agree with our logic or to interpret Scripture in a way that makes the most sense to us.

From that point on, the one who can articulate and prove with traditions or theologians, can move people toward a common belief system, because often times we just want to fit in or find a place that we can live without much effort on our part. It is not easy to grapple with the text or to spend time in prayer, working at discerning or communicating with others to get to the truth of God. Even after that great battle, we are frequently left more confused than when we began. My contention is that we all come into a situation, consciously or unconsciously, with an expected outcome in mind. Based on our desires or hopes for the moment, we move the experience to drive the results we can live with. The more we bring our agenda, hopes, and desires apart from God, the more we find ourselves spinning circles around what it is that God wants.

We want balance in our thoughts that align with our conclusions. We want what we think is fair instead of coming to God seeking a rhythm. We get into His rhythm when we are more concerned about seeking God's face and His Word for us than seeking what we might think or feel is best for the time.

I turn you to one of the longest discussions concerning God's will throughout the entire Scripture: the story of Job. Here we have a man who has just lost everything, including his children, his wealth, and his health. He is sitting by the fire scratching boils because his skin itches. With him are friends who came to comfort him during his grief and they end up spending 34 chapters arguing over the will of God and what Job must have done to bring him to that place in his life. They debate over what he must do to get out, culminating in Job's defensive arguments to plead his understanding of the fairness or lack of fairness on God's part.

From a philosophical and theological standpoint, these are great arguments. The thoughts are challenging, thoughtful, and are used all the time. The problem I find in this book is that they spent 34 chapters pontificating actions, attitudes, and directions, all with the heart of getting Job out of his situation and moving him into being the successful man everyone believed he was. The motives were right, but completely missed the mark.

If you listen to the arguments, you hear each person believing what they wanted to believe and coming into the argument with their own agenda, their own understanding. Job did not need concerned men telling him what he needed to do to get out of his situation; He needed his friends to simply sit there and be with him; he needed to be with God and hopefully hear His voice, which finally came to all of them in chapter 38. What was God's answer to Job? Did God give him a list of things he did right or wrong? No. Did God give him a master plan on how to get out of his predicament? No. Did God give Job Scripture verses to follow in hopes that he would walk in the right path and discover the truth? No.

What God did was ask questions. Listen to Job 38:1-3, "Then the Lord spoke to Job out of the storm. He said: "Who is this that obscures my plans with words without knowledge? Brace yourself like a man; I will question you, and you shall answer me." How many of us come to people with words without knowledge? I am not talking about knowledge of Scripture, but knowledge of God. How many people are giving answers simply because they know the Bible, but have not heard or experienced the presence of God in that moment?

Having knowledge of Scripture is like coming into a relationship with another person by reading their bio, asking them questions about their life, and saying that you know them. To know someone is to take time to know their heart, their desires, their passions, their mysteries; to walk passionately to where you are in harmony with that person. Only then may you have a clearer understanding of who they are. Until we walk this way, we are simply creating an ideological construct on what we think is right and never coming to understand the rhythm of the person.

How many of us live this way with God? Theology comes when we are willing to seek what He wants, when He wants it, the way He wants it, because He is God. We are simply "His workmanship created in Christ Jesus" (Ephesians 2:10). When we are willing to enter into a rhythm with Jesus, we can discover the voice and passion of God.

Chapter 8
Who is God?

"I AM WHO I AM" (Exodus 3:14).

This seems like a bizarre question if you really think about it. If you are a believer in Jesus and were in a discussion with another believer who asked this question, you might respond, "Who do you think? It is Jesus." But I would ask that question again in light of all the results of mankind, the doctrines that keep believers apart, and the arguments that occur in churches weekly. Some people see church more like a commissary, going because they like the music or the children's program instead of seeing it as a holy place of worship.

I have seen pastors fight over the next new program or the next new gimmick, simply to get people into the chairs. I have heard pastors and congregations say they don't worry about all that stuff, they simply teach Jesus. These congregations teach Jesus, yet at the same time bash the forms of doctrine and beliefs they don't agree with, teaching from the pulpit as if their interpretation is the gospel. I have seen people refused membership because they were not baptized the right way and people shunned from the church because of their lifestyles. People who are not in the same social class as the rest are sometimes excluded when they come to church simply to worship. I could go on stating one example after another, but we would still come to the same question. Who is God? I contend that by looking at the way we treat one another, we are prone to play God, while verbalizing God as being the Creator of the Earth and the Savior of our lives.

Things have not changed for centuries. There is a story known to us as The Good Samaritan. In the time of Christ, Samaritans were seen as unclean, unearthly people, many of whom were half-Jewish and half-Gentile in heritage. They came from a nation that promoted sin and rebellion, known as the Northern Tribes, so the Lord allowed them to be captured by the Assyrians who chose to mix nations together so that no one group held exclusive power. This resulted in mixed racial marriages. Thus the Samaritans, in the eyes of the "true Jew," were considered unclean.

Knowing this, Jesus shared the story about a man who was robbed, beaten, stripped of his clothes, and left lying in a ditch. At various times during the day a priest and a Levite, both godly men who were in a position of authority, passed by and saw him. The Scriptures say they walked by him and the priest even went to the other side of the road. Then a Samaritan, who was treated with disrespect, saw the beaten Jew and showed compassion. In his compassion he made sure the man received care and respect. A man who was disrespected showed more respect than the supposedly "godly men."

Who is your God? It is a question that is answered every day through our actions and attitudes. No matter how we say it, our lives and hearts will reflect the truth of what we believe through our actions. If God is daily part of our every moment, it doesn't matter where we are or who we are with, our hearts will reflect the answer to that question. It is interesting how we have created a life of dichotomies. When I am home I act a certain way and say certain things. When I am at work I act out life differently, and even in church the difference shows. We have learned how to balance our lives so that we can be who we need and want to be. As such, we rationalize our attitudes, actions, and the spirit that dwells in us in that time and place. When we sin we can always say, "We all sin," or "That is what grace is about." We even find the right church that either agrees with what we believe or we simply don't go and say, "God understands."

We strive to balance our minds and hearts so they agree with one another, or we justify where we are by saying, "I can't follow my heart. It always gets me into trouble because my heart is deceitful." Some people shut down their minds to what is right, pure, and just, simply saying, "to heck with the church." Then we go off and live the way we want and ignore the very Word of God that helps us understand that we are creatures of worship, and that we will worship something, either God, ourselves, or a god we create in our minds.

Until we come to the God who says in Exodus 3:14, "I AM WHO I AM" and discover that God reveals Himself—we don't choose who He is. God calls Himself *Yahweh*, not us. We have the privilege of worshipping Him the way He wants us to, believing in Him the way He desires, or to honor our own beliefs and live our own lifestyle. We get to choose, but as a leadership organization taught me, choices come with both consequences and blessings.

After Solomon was king, the Jewish nation was split into two. There was the Northern Kingdom and the Southern Kingdom, each with its own king. The place of worship was in Jerusalem, which was in the Southern Kingdom, so out of fear of losing his kingdom King Jeroboam built two golden calves, placing one in Bethel and the other in Dan. He told the people they could worship in either place, making it easier than traveling all the way to Jerusalem (1 Kings 12:25-33). How convenient and how totally disrespectful of the God we are called to worship.

Who makes the rules? Who tells us who He is? Who created us? Somehow we believe in our hearts that we know what is best for us whether we are Christians or not. So we create a god out of our own ideology and interpret the Law any way we want, worship any way we want, and judge any way we want because it fits with our lifestyle or opinions. When we need help, instead of seeking the face of God and falling to our knees and spending time with Him, we buy a book that will guide us without doing the diligent work of seeking God's face first.

I contend that we have elevated certain authors, pastors, and theologians by placing them on a pedestal because we agree with what they say, and it fits our belief system. When we have more problems we continue to go to those people instead of the Lord. I have bookshelves full of some of the richest theology, wisdom, and insight. I admit it is easy to grab for one of those scholars instead of the Bible; it's easier than wrestling with the Scriptures in my hand, or praying on my knees with a few friends at my side in compassionate understanding, or spending time seeking the face of God and His heart.

I have been in circles where people talk about their pastor or a writer as if he were the god they worship because he has the answers they want. The answers tickle the ear and satisfy the heart for a moment, so they must be right. The reality is that the person we quote, or the pastor we listen to, may have the right answer, but unless he points to God in the person of Jesus Christ, he is only providing a convenient answer rather than the right answer. The gospel is not something we can add to, it is simply the Word of Jesus Christ. Unless I am willing to meet Him daily face to face I will worship other things and seek answers that are not complete.

I have been married for over 30 years and have realized that books can only help me come close to understanding my wife, Cindy, or how I might want to respond to her. The work of a true marriage is a willingness to sit together emotionally naked and feel no shame. Until we are willing to do the work found in the Scriptures alone, our marriages will not be the best we can have. We may have a great marriage, and for some people that is enough, but if we want the best it comes when we sit face to face with each other and with the Word of God, and figure it out with the Spirit of God guiding us.

Books can help and support, but they cannot lead. The Bible and the Spirit of God lead us to the understanding and acknowledgement of the God we need to be worshipping and what that worship should look like. For more than three hundred years there was only one church. It was the gathering of the body, and not a building. The early church met in caves, homes, and in the forest. It was a place that people were willing to lose their lives for the opportunity to visit and worship. Young mothers and men would leave their homes early in the morning and sacrifice rumors and persecution to worship and break bread together in holy communion. They were a group of people connected through their belief system in Jesus Christ, and their authority derived from the letters of Paul and the other Scripture readings where they worked together to find the voice of God.

Once Constantine nationalized the church, it became more of the place to go. The tax money was taken away from other religious organizations and given to the one church, which then became an institution. From that moment on, we lost sight of the church as it was meant to be and it has become splintered by religious beliefs and doctrines all because we have chosen to worship the way we want, when we want, and who we want. Is that the God of the Scripture or of man's thoughts and interpretations? Whom do we worship?

It is not easy, but if we can come to the Lord and seek His face and His Spirit and take time to read His Word and grapple with it, we will come to see the world through the eyes of Christ, with the heart of Christ, and live in the fullness of His Spirit. This comes not in seeking our own rhythm, but in understanding His rhythm and seeing the world as He created it to be. How do we do that effectively? In the next few chapters, I will recommend possible answers that come from His Word.

Chapter 9

Live a Juxtaposed Life

"I am the Lord who exercises kindness, justice, and righteousness on earth" (Jeremiah 9:24b).

No matter how theologically astute, or how old I have become, every time I have Chinese food I grab a fortune cookie and read what my fortune might be. I love it when I get a fortune that resonates with my heart and there is still that small child's spirit in me that wants to believe it will come true. It can, but it doesn't just happen. Whether we want to admit it or not, life takes work. In Christian circles we call it stewardship. The more we steward our time, skill sets, strengths, talents, gifts, and the people around us, the more successful we will become, maybe not in the eyes of the world, but in the eyes of God.

Humans seek comfort and endeavor to make life as easy as possible. As believers we seek God's approval in what we are thinking, feeling, and striving toward. Oftentimes we turn to Scripture verses, poems, or devotionals that resonate with our hearts, or we listen to worship music in hopes that our hearts and God's heart will be in alignment without much agony or struggle.

Without realizing it, we are creating in our lives a look-good, feel-good gospel—one of good fortune, or one that at least satisfies the taste buds of a life that moves us along the pathway to happiness. Now it sounds like I am a naysayer of God's fortune upon us, or of people who are reading devotionals or listening to songs, or even poems that might help us hear the voice of God and His direction for our lives. This is not the case. I am saying that we need to be careful that these tools do not define the gospel for us. It is God who defines the gospel, and sometimes the poems, readings, and songs are our desire for us and not the Lord's. As believers we live this kind of tension. The gospel is clear, but we at times can read it one way or another based on what we seek. I refer to it as tension because everything around the gospel goes against the very desires within us. It is not the gospel of self-preservation, but the gospel of Jesus Christ, and with it comes obedience and devotion to Him, His Law, His words, and His life while learning to lose our own in the process.

We talked earlier about how Christianity is a paradox—a life that calls us to live the opposite of how our natural desires or tensions want us to live. The other part of Christianity that makes life a little harder is the realization that the very things Christ calls us to—to live a life of grace, joy, and faith—are also the same as living in obedience to the Law, seeking justice, and holding one another accountable. Many Christians live on one side of the spectrum or the other. Some just focus on grace, faith, and love, letting God deal with justice, obedience to the Law, and accountability. As such, we simply let other believers suffer in their sin. Or we live as if we are the keepers of what is right and fair and live only in accordance to the Law, and in doing so become those who shoot the wounded.

Most would say that the way through this dilemma is to live a balanced life, but what does that mean? How can you balance law and grace, love and healthy judgment, and mercy and accountability? How can you balance all other aspects of life with Christ, which speaks clearly to a life of tension between the two, without wavering on one side or the other? In other words, how do we live a juxtaposed life, a life that holds the tension between the two, so that we are not erring on either side, but holding the tension in perfect harmony with the Spirit of Christ?

Before we explore how this can be done, let's go to the source of the One who shows us the how, that being Christ Himself. There are many stories that show us the how; I am only going to discuss a few of them.

The first story is in Mark 12:14-17:

> They came to him and said, "Teacher, we know that you are a man of integrity. You aren't swayed by others, because you pay no attention to who they are; but you teach the way of God in accordance with the truth. Is it right to pay the imperial tax to Caesar or not? Should we pay or shouldn't we?" But Jesus knew their hypocrisy. "Why are you trying to trap me?" he asked. "Bring me a denarius and let me look at it." They brought the coin, and he asked them, "Whose image is this? And whose inscription? "Caesar's," they replied. Then Jesus said to them, "Give back to Caesar what is Caesar's and to God what is God's." And they were amazed at him.

In this passage we find the tension between right and wrong, law and grace, justice and mercy, and speaking out of wisdom, not simply knowledge. Upon hearing their question, Jesus asked for a coin. That coin speaks of justice, honor, and what is right and true, whether we agree with it or not. It represented a system of government. Being aware of all of that, as well as their desire to use it to trap Him, Jesus helps us understand the juxtaposed life. He has the ability to hold to what is the world's and what belongs to Him. Giving to Caesar what is Caesar's is right, and giving to the Lord what belongs to the Lord is right, as well. The Lord can hold the tension between the two as He shows us in His Word.

With these words in mind, let's read Exodus and then Romans. Moses penned this statement in Exodus, "I am the Lord your God, who brought you out of Egypt, out of the land of slavery. You shall have no other gods before me" (Exodus 20:2-3).

> Let everyone be subject to the governing authorities, for there is no authority except that which God has established. The authorities that exist have been established by God. Consequently, whoever rebels against the authority is rebelling against what God has instituted, and those who do so will bring judgment on themselves. For rulers hold no terror for those who do right, but for those who do wrong. Do you want to be free

> from fear of the one in authority? Then do what is right and you will be commended. For the one in authority is God's servant for your good. But if you do wrong, be afraid, for rulers do not bear the sword for no reason. They are God's servants, agents of wrath to bring punishment on the wrongdoer. Therefore, it is necessary to submit to the authorities, not only because of possible punishment but also as a matter of conscience (Romans 13:1-5).

Here you find the tension of honoring authority and understanding that what we think and feel is decided ultimately by God. If our hearts and minds are in sync with the Lord, we will choose the right person to lead; if not, God still allows the choice and the blessings or consequences that are ours. Our allegiance gets messed up when we put our devotion in the things of the world and not in the Lord. Whether it is the things of the world or the things that hold our religious belief together, when we serve those things we fall into the place of worshipping something other than God Himself.

Our devotion and allegiance needs to be in God, not to religious or political practices—not in what is going to give me the greatest tax break or meet the social causes of the world. When we are in sync with the Lord and seek Him first, we can see things more clearly and respond in the Holy Spirit and not our spirit.

The third story that shows us the juxtaposed life of a believer is in John 8:1-11:

> But Jesus went to the Mount of Olives. At dawn he appeared again in the temple courts, where all the people gathered around him, and he sat down to teach them. The teachers of the law and the Pharisees brought in a woman caught in adultery. They made her stand before the group and said to Jesus, "Teacher, this woman was caught in the act of adultery. In the Law Moses commanded us to stone such women. Now what do you say?" They were using this question as a trap, in order to have a basis for accusing him. But Jesus bent down and started to write on

> the ground with his finger. When they kept on questioning him, he straightened up and said to them, "Let any one of you who is without sin be the first to throw a stone at her." Again he stooped down and wrote on the ground. At this, those who heard began to go away one at a time, the older ones first, until only Jesus was left, with the woman still standing there. Jesus straightened up and asked her, "Woman, where are they? Has no one condemned you?" "No one, sir," she said. "Then neither do I condemn you," Jesus declared. "Go now and leave your life of sin."

In this passage we see a huge divergent tension between the Law in Leviticus 20:10 which says, "If a man commits adultery with another man's wife—with the wife of his neighbor—both the adulterer and the adulteress are to be put to death," and the words of Matthew 5:27-30:

> "You have heard that it was said, 'You shall not commit adultery.' But I tell you that anyone who looks at a woman lustfully has already committed adultery with her in his heart. If your right eye causes you to stumble, gouge it out and throw it away. It is better for you to lose one part of your body than for your whole body to be thrown into hell. And if your right hand causes you to stumble cut it off and throw it away. It is better for you to lose one part of your body than for your whole body to go into hell."

I have heard many different explanations for all three passages as people try to reconcile them in the minds of listeners and readers alike. We want either to know what the rules are so we can live accordingly, or we want to do what we want, dealing with the consequences later. What Jesus is showing us is that each situation in life has to be discerned by the Spirit. If we try to find one concrete answer for all circumstances, we are going to make mistakes which may cause others to stumble and fall instead of our being the vessels God can use for restorative purposes.

This does not mean that life is relative and can be translated as we go. It simply means that we, as believers, live in the Spirit of Christ and are willing to test ourselves not in congruence with popular opinion, but with people who agree with the Spirit of God. This occasionally leads us to an uncomfortable place, as these may be people we do not like or agree with in normal situations. It is the Spirit of God that moves as He wills, and in whom.

We tend to be drawn to people who agree with us or whom we can talk into agreeing with us. This is not the Spirit; hearing the Spirit of God comes through times of testing, fasting, reading, and praying. Too often we do not take the time to find the rhythm that gives us God's answer. Instead we take the easy way out, finding someone who communicates with us God's opinion based on their studies, and because that person is a leader, we believe it must be from the Lord.

How then does one live a juxtaposed life and seek the Kingdom of God and His righteousness? The key is in the heart of the believer. We simply have to ask ourselves: is the person who is talking actually walking and living a humble and obedient life in the ways of God? One way to discern is to listen to the person as he talks about the Lord.

Incongruity can be seen where pastors give great sermons about restoration, teaching: we are restored in the grace and arms of God for His good service. That same pastor may then turn around and reject someone from serving in the church because that person has had a divorce or an affair, or has been involved in pornography. A church may also say that the communion table is open to all believers, but because a person is living a certain way they go to 1 Corinthians 11 to validate their refusal to serve them communion instead of taking time to embrace that brother or sister to help them see God's forgiveness by coming to the table of life with believers around them.

Congruency is not only living a life that looks good, but a life that truly speaks of the passion of Christ as if Christ were present in the conversation. If you are a believer in Jesus Christ and are open to the Spirit, you will hear and see the Spirit of Christ in someone else, even if you don't agree with what they are saying. In that conversation you can see the hands, face, and words of Christ, which may go against what you are thinking and feeling.

Hold the tension by living in the Spirit, being bathed in His Spirit, and staying rooted in prayer and His Word. In the situation, allow yourself to recall all you know, feel, and experience. When you are seeking the Kingdom first and foremost, then the things and answers you seek truly will come into being, out of your being in Christ our Lord. It is in that tension that we discover the Great I AM.

Chapter 10
The Great I AM

"Who do you say I am?" (Mark 8:29).

For a time I wore a button that said, "Accept your greatness." I rarely received any comments about it until I went to a place of worship. Sadly, when I was there the comments were not very positive. I would either see people read it and walk away or hear the comment, "There is nothing about me that is great, only Jesus." My heart cried for those people. I wanted to say to them, "If there is nothing great about you then why would God take the trouble to die for you?"

Jesus died for us because He decided we were worth saving. Jesus died because what He created was good. Jesus died because according to David in Psalm 139:14 we are fearfully and wonderfully made. I could be overreacting to their comment about my button, or am I? What gives the cross its value is that God saw value in us, and He did not want it to be washed away throughout eternity.

Does this mean that I should walk around prideful and arrogant, puffing myself up because I am great? Absolutely not, because without Christ that greatness is simply temporal and isolated to the value I place in it. With the help of His saving blood and adopting us as sons and daughters, our value exceeds any and every thing that we can do on our own.

What I am describing is the tension that resides within us, and with that tension comes the awareness of God, or our lack of awareness of the true God, Who longs for us to see Him as He is. This also means that we need to see ourselves the way God sees us and not the way we believe on our own.

The clearer picture we have of this, the greater our opportunity to see things and respond out of rhythm rather than trying to reach a balance. Some people reason, "The greater I see myself, the less I depend on God" or "The less I see in me, the more I need Him." However, this perspective is in contradiction to how we should think; it is not what I think about myself, but how does the Lord want me to see Him and me that matters.

With this thought in mind, let's look at God as He describes Himself to Moses. When God asked Moses to be the leader of more than three million people, he was a bit distraught. So much so that he went to God and asked, "Who do I say sent me?" God responded, "Tell them, I AM sent you."

Though often misunderstood, it is important to accept that Christ's death did not make us special; we *are* special because everything God does He does in love. Christ's death made us complete in Him without sin to block our awareness of who He is and who we are in His sight. Once we are there, we can see for ourselves that God is love. He doesn't *do* love; He *is* love. That's His state of being. He is grace; He is justice; He is purity; and He is holy. So, when Moses asks how God defines Himself, the answer is, "I AM WHO I AM." We don't hold the existence of *Yahweh* with the power and intensity that it deserves. God doesn't *do* love; God *is* love. God doesn't show mercy; He *is* mercy. Everything He does, He does in mercy and justice; He holds the tension equal. That fact just doesn't make sense to most people. Some might ask, "Then why would He kill millions of people?" He didn't kill millions of people, SIN killed millions of people. Man's disobedience killed millions of people. How could God allow AIDS? Because God allowed mankind to make a choice and mankind chose it. As one person once said, "Choices have costs, and they have benefits." Man continues to choose sin, and man continues to search for a God who shows love the way we want Him to show it, instead of searching for a God who *is* love.

You are a manifestation of His love. You are a manifestation of being special. You are whole and complete; wonderful, powerful, and dynamic. You are! That is the way God created us to be. When you go and just *be*, you can be those things. You can also be obnoxious, rude, self-centered and egotistical. What drives the existence of those actions? Your beingness! You've equated or attached labels to beingness, but they are not your beingness. They are attributes that come out of your beingness, and that beingness is driven by the very essence of who you are, whether it's your self-centeredness or the revelation of the God who dwells in you.

God says, "I AM WHO I AM." What do you do with that? What did Moses do with it? He journeyed to Egypt and said, "Let my people go, or the Lord will strike you." Where did that come from? How did it come into being? How could Moses do and say what he did? It was because he allowed God to *be*, and in that being multitudes of things happened. Why Moses? Moses was willing to listen; he simply did what God asked of him and believed the God who revealed His love through a fire by night and a cloud by day. Out of who He is, He parted the waters and provided manna and quail. He showed how disobedience to Him and people's sin was unacceptable by allowing serpents to kill them; and at the same time for those who repented and sought His way, He provided a serpent on a stick and they were healed. God was and is and always will be because it's a part of His beingness; the freedom we have is the privilege to choose it or ignore it. Our response is not up to God, it is up to us. The costs and benefits are simply consequences of the choices we have made, or that have been made by someone else. We are living in the fallout of those choices.

God's response will always be the same, because Jesus is the same yesterday, today, and forever. (Hebrews 13:8) God does not change because of who we are, what we want, or how we want it. God does intervene in *kairos* moments, in Holy God times. He shows up because He anointed it before the act takes place. We see it and feel it because we are more receptive than at any other moment. You could be in a *kairos* moment right now if you are receptive and responsive to Who He is, not what He does. How do we take the "I AM" into our day? *Just be.* Savor the moments as they come. Who knows what He has in store for you?

Most of us do things or set goals because we want to accomplish something, instead of realizing we are accomplished. Out of that accomplishment we can step into areas of our lives to manifest and reflect that accomplishment. What do you need to embrace at this moment? *Just be*. You deserve to be all that you are in front of people.

Say these words out loud until you believe them: "I am at my fullest in Him."

Prayer

Holy Father, I thank You for the love that flows because You are. For the mercy You give because You are. For the tenderness and the discipline and the judgment that falls because You are. As I sit and embrace Your Beingness, I know that I am affected by it, which makes me who I am. The more I embrace the You that You have shown for centuries, the more I can stand in Your Beingness and in mine and be empowered, whatever that moment might look like. So help me transcend my doctrines, my theologies, my ideologies, my comfort or lack of comfort, my dependence or my independence. Help me to simply just be, and out of that beingness may I find harmony in all that I say and do because of Who You are and Who You are in me.

May an extraordinary thing happen as a result of this today, to bring all of this to the concrete, to the foundation of my beingness. Lord, I pray that I will be healed of what keeps getting in the way of what You want because I am so focused on what I think You want me to have or what I want for myself. Help me see that You are. And in that may I find Your rhythm—Your movement. God, help me transcend from stories and images of the past in my life and the things that keep me from thinking and feeling differently from what You seek for me. Help me to see that life is about glorifying You and You alone—the You that is imparted in my being and in my deliverance from sin, shame, guilt, and blame. Help me see that every room in my heart is completely exposed and gutted and only You reside. Help me hear You, know You, feel You, and be embraced by You, for it's You that matters, and may my beingness come as a result of who You are. In Jesus' Name, Amen!

Chapter 11

Embracing Hope

"And hope does not put us to shame, because God's love has been poured out into our hearts through the Holy Spirit, who has been given to us" (Romans 5:5).

In 1834 a gentleman by the name of Edward Mote wrote the lyrics to a song that has been sung by generations of people. The first stanza and chorus read:

My hope is built on nothing less
Than Jesus' blood and righteousness;
I dare not trust the sweetest frame,
But wholly lean on Jesus' name.

Refrain:
On Christ, the solid Rock, I stand;
All other ground is sinking sand,
All other ground is sinking sand.

These words have echoed through the chambers of buildings throughout the world. They are hummed and sung in the most disappointing times and in times that people desire to proclaim their faith and assurance on Him.

It is a song that speaks of hope—hope in God Himself—who came to Earth some 2,000 years ago and died for us. Hope in Jesus as God, Lord, and Savior. The question that moves me into this chapter as we explore a theology that God shows us versus an ideology that we create in our own minds is, "What does hope really look like?" What does it mean to have hope in Jesus? How does that help me through my day when I am trying to understand why a loved one just committed suicide, why the Lord would allow me to lose my job after 25 years in the same place, or why I feel I have done everything to save my marriage that ends in divorce because my spouse has left me for another? What does hope feel like when I am sitting in the doctor's office and I hear for the first time that I have cancer, or that my child has leukemia?

How can you have hope in a God to Whom you pray to heal your child, your marriage, your livelihood, and your life, yet things only appear to get worse? How do we handle it when we are in pain, feeling darkness all around us, and another well-meaning Christian tries to show sympathy by sharing the story of Job, and all we want to do is cram that story in the person's face "in a Christian way?"

Hope is one of those words that is used as much as "love" and "faith," yet for many people it seems to take a distant second to the words "pain" and "survival." Optimists and pastors alike speak about it, sing about it, share about it, but often we do not take the time to look at God's view point of what it looks like to live out hope, no matter what we are facing. It is not a principle that we can simply go to church and find like we can go to a store and get a gallon of milk. Hope is something that we experience out of a relationship that is rich and real. The richer the relationship the more we see and experience the hope that is ours.

It starts with receiving Christ as our Lord and Savior, but it is much more than simply praying to receive Christ and acknowledging that we are sinners. The apostle Paul unpacks the understanding of hope in Romans 5:1-5 this way:

> Therefore, since we have been justified through faith, we have peace with God through our Lord Jesus Christ, through whom

> we have gained access by faith into this grace in which we now stand. And we boast in the hope of the glory of God. Not only so, but we also glory in our sufferings, because we know that suffering produces perseverance; perseverance, character; and character, hope. And hope does not put us to shame, because God's love has been poured out into our hearts through the Holy Spirit, who has been given to us.

I have discussed this passage with many people over the years as they found themselves struggling or discouraged. My desire was that the Word of God might bring them comfort. To some it does, because the Spirit of God soothes their soul at the time. What Paul is saying is that we as believers can stand in the hope of His glory and find peace through our Lord Jesus Christ because life is not about the circumstances we are facing or the struggles we are encountering, it is about having hope in God. The more we persevere, the stronger our character will reflect His character. The more we experience God in our character, the more others see Him and the more hope we feel, because we become increasingly awakened by His presence in our lives as our character yields more to His character in and through us.

These words have been flying out of my mind for years. I have preached them, shared them with others, and prayed for hope. So often I found the hope I experienced was short-lived. It eluded me not because I did not have God in my life, but because I was looking in the wrong place in order to find it.

To understand this more clearly I want to revisit the story of Job which is a book about suffering and blessings. The book of Job is about how a righteous, loving God could allow a man to lose everything when in the eyes of the world he did nothing wrong. To others, it is about four friends who tried to help Job through his suffering and pain. Most of the book is a discussion of why Job suffered such tragedies and how his problems could be rectified. The book ends with God challenging Job, his resolve to serve God, and finally a blessing for him.

As I ponder this passage again, I think about how they kept trying to offer suggestions, like any good friends would. Each time, Job had a rebuttal, and his friends came back with their own understanding. From verse eleven in chapter two, all the way through to chapter thirty-seven, Job and his friends were batting around this dilemma, and finally God intervened in chapter thirty-eight. What was the purpose of all that discussion? There are several possibilities, but I want to focus on one; without those conversations, we may have never discovered hope.

It wasn't until I was writing this chapter and talking to a great friend about hope and Job that I saw it staring me in the face. Most of us have these types of discussions because we're trying to understand—trying to find the answers to our problems so we can move on with our lives. We seek the end result—the goal, and to find it we look at blame, shame, guilt, and the sins of our fathers. There must be a reason that makes sense, and once we have that rational reason we will develop a plan to move forward. When we sin, we pray for forgiveness. Let's figure out what sin created the death of a child. Let's blame our parents, or Adam, for allowing my teenage son to commit suicide. When we don't blame sin, we use psychology; we need to find the cause of this problem so we can come up with the solution. I am not trying to bash science or the influence of sin; however, the point I am making here is we want a solution so we can have the answer. It is the answer that we believe will get us out of the dilemma and give us hope.

We desperately want answers that allow us to make sense of things to help us resolve issues and struggles. We live for the answers. Our hope lies in the answers, not in the person of God. We have to be careful with this, otherwise we become like the disciples in their naiveté asking the question about a blind man in John 9:2, "Who sinned, this man or his parents, that he was born blind?" Or like Job when God was asking him questions. If we are open to the Lord, it is in the questions that we can discover hope as the disciples and Job did. His response is recorded:

> Then Job replied to the Lord: "I know that you can do all things; no purpose of yours can be thwarted You asked, 'Who is this that obscures my plans without knowledge?' Surely I spoke of things I did not understand, things too wonderful for me to know" (Job 42:2-3).

What I saw was that Job's answer wasn't in the knowledge; it was in the person of *Yahweh*. Years ago I read a book by Basil Pennington titled ***Living the Questions***. To this day it remains one of my favorite reads. He helped me discover the concept of living in the question. Throughout the New Testament, Jesus asks one question after another. To Andrew and the other disciple He asks, "What do you want?" (John 1:37) To Peter and the other disciples He asks, "Who do you say I am?" (Matthew 16:15) To the Pharisees He inquires, "Have you never read what David did when he and his companions were hungry?" (Luke 6:3) Through His questions, Jesus provided not the answers His audience sought, but rather a redirection to the truth.

It is not the answers that God wants us to experience and live out, it is in the Person of Jesus Christ that we find hope. It is in His character, and in allowing that character to dwell in us, we can truly live out the hope of God. Hope is not found in the construct or a verse; it is found in the Person of Jesus, Who is hope.

Now we can begin to understand that the fullness that flows between man and God is not the answer to our problems or sufferings. It is not about the reward that Job received at the end of suffering; it is not about how we discover who we are in relation to God. The relationship is about fulfillment and love, which comes in the hope we have in Him. God is our fulfillment through Christ our Lord. It takes that relationship to discover true hope. We want that union in which we feel the love of God in the difficult times as well as the good times. Guess what?! It will never happen until—and here's the golden nugget—the person is willing to know the heart of God the way God wants His heart to be known. This is not achieved by seeking the answers, but by learning to live in the questions of life and finding Him, Who is hope.

Isn't that what we want? Don't we want people to know us for who we really are and not who they think we are? Why is God any different if we are made in His image? Why do we say, "Let me tell you what God's heart looks like" and base it on our experiences instead of really getting to know His heart? The answer to God's heart is in the Scriptures. People can give us their interpretation of what it says, even to the point of bringing clarity to our hearts and thoughts, but the fullness of the truth comes when we ask God what He says.

How do you properly express the words, "God is hope, keep looking to Him" without a formula; without some translation? To illustrate, let's examine a line from Psalm 23:4, "Yea though I walk through the valley of the shadow of death, I will fear no evil" (NKJV). What does that actually mean? There is the awareness that God is leading and an awareness of the valley of the shadow of death. The imagery is that during the summer months they moved the sheep from the valley to the mountaintop where there was rich, green grass from the winter moisture that had saturated the soil. They brought the sheep down from the mountain to the valley in the winter because the mountaintop would freeze. When he says, "though I walk through the valley of the shadow of death," he's talking about the narrow pathways to reach their destination. The lambs could easily make one wrong step and tumble down the cliff, so they stayed tight and did exactly what the shepherd did to get through the valley into the green pastures. It's a great image.

God gave us the formula, not the how to's, and that's the problem. It's not about how to's—"you pray more, you reach more," "you give more, you get more," and so on—and it's not about what we do. It's about realizing that if you *be* this person, this begins to happen. That's the context of this book, BE THIS PERSON AND THE RIGHT THINGS WILL HAPPEN. When you are being this person, the revelation is there; it comes in the being, not in the doing.

Hope is ours if we are willing to be what God desires us to be and live as God desires us to live. This is about getting to know Him each and every day. That is where we find hope, because we find God. Once we've discovered the God Who created the heavens and the earth, we discover how big He is.

Chapter 12

How Big is Your God?

"Where were you when I laid the earth's foundation? Tell me, if you understand" (Job 38:4).

This title may offend some people because we all want to believe we are seeing God the way He wants us to see Him. We all have conceptions of who He is or who He isn't. We have all created in our hearts and minds the way in which we see Him, and we all want our way to be right. For those of you who may be offended, this chapter was written for you. It is not intended to offend, but rather to help you see that too often the way we see God is our way and not His.

Take, for instance, the groups of Jewish officials known as the Pharisees and the Sadducees. These Jewish leaders grew out of the time of the inter-testament period. They were the watchdogs of Jewish society at a time when living a certain way was governed by Jewish Law. Even though they believed in *Yahweh* they had different interpretations about how to live out the Law in its principles and conduct. As a result, they opposed each other until Jesus came on to the scene, and they discovered that they opposed Jesus more than they did each other. The outcome was that their rage for Jesus was stronger than their dislike for each other, so they joined forces. We read in the book of Matthew:

> The Pharisees and Sadducees came to Jesus and tested him by asking him to show them a sign from heaven. He replied, "When evening comes, you say, 'It will be fair weather, for the sky is red,' and in the morning, 'Today it will be stormy, for the sky is red and overcast.' You know how to interpret the appearance of the sky, but you cannot interpret the signs of the times. A wicked and adulterous generation looks for a sign, but none will be given it except the sign of Jonah." Jesus then left them and went away (Matthew 16:1-4).

Think about this for a moment. We have two groups of Jewish leaders not unlike denominational leaders of today. Because of the differences in their understanding, they did not associate with each other and both believed they were right in their interpretation. Then there came a common cause for the Pharisees and Sadducees; Jesus became a threat to the status quo, and He was a threat to them. He was perceived as taking away their authority, so they pulled together and challenged Jesus on His wisdom about heaven.

How many times have we heard arguments and seen congregations split over issues like baptism, communion, pads in the pews, music in the sanctuary, or lack of certain music? Each group believes they are right. The Pharisees and Sadducees were so angry at Jesus that they could not even think straight. They were the officials who held the truth of the commandments, even the command which forbids us to have any other god before us (Exodus 20:2-3). How many people have made their understanding of the Word or their understanding of doctrine to be their god? I can hear people responding to this as I type, "I do not view my doctrine to be god!" Yet if we carefully look at the whole of Scripture and the history of mankind, we see bloody battles over doctrinal issues; even today we are split over interpretations. People embrace their doctrine and their religious beliefs as the right ones. Christians argue over baptism, the death penalty, grace and law, accountability, and many other issues. If others do not believe what we do, we simply discard them from our inner circle and do not associate with them. Isn't that what was in the hearts and minds of the Jewish officials in Jesus' time? Didn't they even use the word blasphemer? Look throughout history at the number of crusades fought for religious freedom and purposes.

I contend that we fight these wars and have these arguments so we can reach a balance between what we are feeling and what we are thinking. As such, we create a movement to support wanting what we want, when we want, and how we want it. We do not want to appear self-centered or self-focused, so we couch it in the environment of theology, atheism, or agnosticism to support what we think we need. Thus, we create a god (even those who deny there is a God) of our own image rather than allowing God to help us reveal His image to us and in us.

Leaving the theological arguments for a moment, I want to share how I believe this comes about in our lives. I grew up in a very conservative protestant denominational church. I was told that we sang *a cappella* because musical instruments were not mentioned as being used in the New Testament for worship; therefore, we did not use them in our worship services. We sang Psalms rather than hymns because Psalms were right out of Scripture, whereas man wrote hymns. When we associated with other believers as a church, it was only with people from the same denomination who believed the same as we did. We had our own community and did not associate with other believers who held opposing interpretations. I believe this statement is implied in every church today: my belief about God and how He wants us to live is right and I can support it through Scripture. This was never said, but the implication was ever-present.

In my senior year of high school I liked a particular girl who invited me to her church, which was a charismatic church. They had a band, spoke in tongues, marched in the aisles, and danced in the Spirit. The first time I went, I was blown away and frozen in my seat. I never realized anything like this existed in the Christian faith. I began to understand just how big and embracing God can be. I did not stay in that church, nor did I stay in the church of my childhood. Though I have been educated and trained in the reformed tradition, even today I attend a non-denominational church whose doctrine disagrees with the traditions I was trained to support and defend.

People tend to create boxes for their conceptions of God. We don't call them boxes, but they are nice denominational or non-denominational precepts that conform to our beliefs at that moment, and we support and argue them as though they are right. In reality, what we truly want is to feel the love, presence, and support of God.

I believe our views are muddled as we have a misunderstanding of need versus want. I did not realize this until I saw it in my personal life. We live as if we are seeking needs. We even tell ourselves that we need this and that; depending on our emotional attachment to that need, we are driven to fulfill what we think is a need. Oftentimes, we even go so far as to say, "I need to be needed." We bring that mindset into our theology and our service so we create a theological ideology only to support that need which sometimes is the need to be right.

This never hit me so hard as when I talked to someone who felt he needed to be needed. I asked him, "Does God need us or want us?" He almost said need, but he stopped and realized that we have substituted the word "need" for "want." The conversation got me thinking about my own life, and I discovered that when I seek what I think is a need, whether it be food, a new electronic gadget, or even a spiritual connection with God, I do whatever I can to obtain that need. When I get it, I am delighted and feel blessed for the moment; it is a high like one might get from sugar.

Then there are times when I am in my stuff, have turned my focus away from God to myself, and move to a place of depression which is fed by blame, shame, and guilt. In those times I feel the desire to be wanted. In those moments I respond to my feelings, which translate into needs. Without realizing it, what I really want is for someone or something to change the way I'm feeling. When I look at my life and my relationship with God in the context of how I got there, I had an amazing revelation: the memories most dear to me are not the ones in which I have been needed, but the ones in which I have been wanted. The reason I mixed wants and needs is that as a human I seek the quick fix, the instant high, that moment of ecstasy when I am excited and feel special. Being wanted doesn't give us that same instant high. It is more like processing proteins in our system that are the last to be digested, but are the most sustainable for our bodies.

What does this have to do with theology and putting God in a box? The more we translate our wants as needs, whether it be the desire to be right, to be in the right place, or to have our wants met, the more we seek them as needs and then create a god that fits those needs at the moment. If those wants continue to be met in that way, we will continue to argue our case whether we are right or wrong.

This brings us back to the Jewish leaders in the time of Jesus. They had a desire for power and to be right, so they used the most powerful weapon they had as a club, their beliefs. What they were doing was creating a theological ideology that supported their desire to be right. What did they really want in life? As I have said before, I do not pretend to be a psychologist, but based on my understanding of Scripture and what I know about humanity, I would venture to say what they wanted was to be just that, wanted. We all want to be wanted for something. The Lord Himself reminds us in the Gospel of John that we are His friends; He chooses us, and the Father validates that relationship by calling us sons and daughters. We are no longer seen as believers, but as sons and daughters. God wants us. Feel that, come to embrace the feeling that comes from that relationship. It will change the way you think and feel for the rest of your life.

When we are wanted, we can look at everything we do not through the eyes of "He needs me," but "He wants me." Our actions are now empowered out of want and not need. Needs for us are conditional and our emotions reflect that. I have seen church members become burned out because they felt needed and abused; they were not getting their personal needs met. You may think I'm splitting hairs here, but how we interpret God wanting us versus needing us changes who we are and why we do things. When I am needed, I justify the energy I give and the sacrifice I am willing to make because there is something in it for me. My sinful nature interprets what I am wanting as a need. When I don't encounter my desired feelings, I interpret that as I am no longer needed.

When I see things through the eyes of wants I can begin to see more clearly how my feelings remain my feelings. If I get tired of serving, helping, or giving advice, I can assimilate it better because I no longer associate what I am doing as a need but a want. When I find myself in a situation in which I am no longer wanted, it is because I was needed for that particular task. When I attach a need to that task it is easier for me to make the situation about me and not about the task.

This sounds very self-centered and me-istic, but without knowing it we do the same with our understanding of God. As long as I interpret God needing me to serve Him, I find it easier to make every decision about me. When I discover how much God wants me, I can choose more powerfully to serve Him as a response to His love. When I see God through the lens of Him needing me, I can easily assume that my act of kindness deserves a blessing, or acknowledgement. When I want to serve Him, it comes out of a desire. It does not matter what I receive in return because it is something I want to do.

Our being is designed and created to want God. As we listen to the Psalmist we hear, "My soul yearns, even faints, for the courts of the LORD; my heart and my flesh cry out for the living God" (Psalm 84:2). In Psalm 42:1-3, we read:

> As the deer pants for streams of water, so my soul pants for you, my God. My soul thirsts for God, for the living God. When can I go and meet with God? My tears have been my food day and night, while people say to me all day long, "Where is your God?"

We play games with God, trying to be in charge—trying to believe that He needs us. We build up our sense of worth and value, when all along our soul wants God. The great news is He wants us. In that want, He longs for us to be in fellowship with Him, walk with Him, and talk with Him. We have the privilege of listening and serving, laughing and rejoicing, and glorifying Him in the workplace and on the home front. We honor His glory through the stewardship of His resources, raising the gifts He gives us in children and nurturing the blessings of friendships. We can treat our bodies like the temple of the Holy Spirit and serve Him with whatever skills and capabilities He has instilled in us.

My Lord wants you and me so much that He died in order that we can dine with Him (Revelation 3:20). When we make it about us and not about Him—when we have lost the power of want—we minimize the relationship and His involvement in our lives.

Maybe we're not putting God in a box because of want versus need, but maybe it is because we simply lack the worth to speak out for Him and His relationship with us. Or maybe it is because our pride cannot accept the true value of who we are in the eyes of God, so we create the relationship in our image. Either way, until we understand how much He longs for us to want Him, we downsize the relationship and what He seeks to do in our lives through His power. This power is diminished when we quench the Holy Spirit and prevent Him from doing what He wants to do in and through us.

We have a tendency to continue seeking that perfect balance in hoping to create our desires. As soon as we realize that our relationship with our big God is not about us, but only about Him, can we see and praise His glory as we enter His rhythm and pattern for our lives.

Chapter 13
No One But You

My vision of God is dependent upon the condition of my character. My character determines whether or not truth can even be revealed to me. Before I can say, "I saw the Lord," there must be something in my character that conforms to the likeness of God. Until I am born again and really begin to see the kingdom of God, I only see from the perspective of my own biases. What I need is God's surgical procedure—His use of external circumstances to bring about internal purification.

Your priorities must be God first, God second, and God third, until your life is continually face to face with God and no one else is taken into account whatsoever. Your prayer will then be, "In all the world there is no one but You, dear God; there is no one but You" (Oswald Chambers, ***My Utmost for His Highest***, July 13).

How do you deal with perfection? Some people say there is no such thing, but that is probably just an excuse to not put our best foot forward and reach out as we obtain the perfection that is offered in Christ. By perfectionism, I am referring to the mindset that people think they are better than others because of their actions or lack of actions. It comes from a place of pride filled with a misunderstanding that a believer ought to look and act a certain way or else their salvation will be questioned. It is a place where we put a lot of emphasis on works, not on love, grace and a deep sense of beingness in Christ.

If we are honest with ourselves most of us believe that no one is perfect, but we still live our lives thinking and feeling that we are better than others. Whether we want to admit it or not, we live in this "state of perfection" based on what we do and do not do as believers in hopes that our lives emulate that of Christ. In the book of Philippians, the apostle Paul talks about coming to this state of perfection or righteousness in Christ alone. In Philippians 3:7-9 we read:

> But whatever were gains to me I now consider loss for the sake of Christ. What is more, I consider everything a loss because of the surpassing worth of knowing Christ Jesus my Lord, for whose sake I have lost all things. I consider them garbage, that I may gain Christ and be found in him, not having a righteousness of my own that comes from the law, but that which is through faith in Christ—the righteousness that comes from God on the basis of faith.

This righteousness is to be seen as a state of being declared righteous not a righteousness that comes from our actions or attitudes—which the apostle Paul calls garbage. Until Paul's conversion under the lordship of Jesus Christ he, like most non-believers, thought all he needed to do was live out the Law as close to perfection as possible. He speaks of this in terms of confidence:

> If someone else thinks they have reasons to put confidence in the flesh, I have more: circumcised on the eighth day, of the people of Israel, of the tribe of Benjamin, a Hebrew of Hebrews; in regard to the law, a Pharisee; as for zeal, persecuting the church; as for righteousness based on the law, faultless (Philippians 3:4b-6).

The apostle Paul had confidence in his own faith and belief in God because he obeyed the Law as perfectly as possible just as many strive to do today. We may say we believe in grace, mercy, and forgiveness, but if we are truly honest with ourselves we realize that many times believers are known to shoot their wounded based on this false conception that one person is better than another, or more perfect than another. Paul realized how absurd that belief system was once Christ was in Him. You see, perfection in life is not about what we do or what we believe, but what we are willing to receive. Once we have received Christ, we become perfect in Him. Being God, He is perfect, and now His perfection lives in us.

Paul goes on to say in this same chapter:

> Not that I have already obtained all this, or have already arrived at my goal, but I press on to take hold of that for which Christ Jesus took hold of me. Brothers and sisters, I do not consider myself yet to have taken hold of it. But one thing I do: Forgetting what is behind and straining toward what is ahead, I press on toward the goal to win the prize for which God has called me heavenward in Christ Jesus (Philippians 3:12-14).

He realized that perfection is only obtained by experiencing what Christ experienced through His physical death and resurrection. Paul also realized that we were given the ability to live our lives to please and glorify God in all that we do. Because of who Christ is, we are made perfect. The more we understand who He is and the more we yield our lives to the work of the Holy Spirit who dwells in us, the more He allows us to live up to the expectations of the Father, which moves us toward perfection. Again, we cannot do this alone. We must yield to what God is doing in and through us. The work we do appears to be coming out of us, but it is the work of the Holy Spirit through us.

This brings us back to the realization that perfection is not in our knowing, but in our being. When we step into being the person the Lord created us to be, guided by His presence and power, the revelation of the gospel will appear. This does not mean that we don't spend time getting to know the Lord through His Word, prayer, and life challenges, but in so doing we are willing to enter into a relationship in which He is directing us and revealing Himself.

One day I was speaking with a friend who was having challenges with his son which caused problems in his relationship with the Lord. This man had been a believer for years, gone to church, and read the Bible from time to time. In his mind and heart, he had done all the right things. Yet, somehow he still felt disconnected. How many people walk the walk, know about the Bible, accept Christ like the church has shared with them, and have been baptized, but walk through life feeling they are simply going through the motions and not seeing the fruit of their relationship with our Lord? I contend that these people know about the Lord, but do not know the Lord. In essence they have become "institutionalized," like those who live in prison for years and learn to follow the rules in order to stay out of trouble, but become lost upon their release. The world has changed, and they have chosen to simply follow the ways of others, thinking it's necessary for survival. Without the direction of others, they are not sure what to do next.

This may appear judgmental to some, but how many believers today are "institutionalized?" How many believers are relying on the pastor or the church doctrine to tell them how to experience and know God? How many people turn to others when they struggle for the answers instead of learning how to have a real relationship with the One who will be there no matter what? I have served the Lord most of my life, but for most of those years I served him with a servant mindset instead of understanding the sonship that was rightfully mine from the time I was nine years old. Many times, I had gone for days on end trying to feel and experience the love of God. I did all the right things. I read daily, prayed constantly, and spent my life sharing how much the Lord loved each and every person around me. For some reason that feeling of love was off and on for me, and the more I served the more distant I felt.

Several years ago I discovered just how much I was serving out of obedience and not out of the love that He had for me. God had been communicating His love all my life, but I never felt it on a consistent basis; it seemed conditional. I had to reach rock bottom and be honest with myself and others in order to truly understand God's unconditional love for me. I am His son. I am obedient to His Word, not because I have to be or am supposed to be, but because of His love. When I was open to discover the God who had been trying to reveal Himself to me my whole life, and not focused on doctrine or scholars who I loved and admired, I was finally able to recognize and receive His love.

I came to appreciate those scholars and the church while enjoying getting to know the One who first loved me and gave His life for me. The more I became a participant in the gospel and yielded my ways to His and my thoughts to His as the prophet Isaiah encourages, the more I accepted my sonship. The more I get to know and love God, the God who calls me His son, the same God I had tried to get to know and serve my way, the more I've embraced the fellowship, the love, and the relationship He offers to all of us.

The more we are willing to yield our lives, our ways, and our thoughts to His, the more we can grasp how wide and deep the love of Christ is for us. Not because we are sinners and He died for us, but because He wants a real relationship with us as we have with others. We need to realize that a real relationship with God is not one based on what He can or desires to do for us. A real relationship comes from getting to know Him and being a part of His life as He desires to be in ours.

The Perfect Bite

A real relationship with God is like experiencing the perfect bite. We all have one, whether we realize it or not. It is that one bite of food that mixes together in our mouth and gives us a sense of heaven as we experience the taste and smell. Our senses come together at that moment and the world stops. For some, that perfect bite is Merlot and chocolate, or a fresh crab and cheddar melt with avocado. For others it is the middle bite of a sandwich where all the ingredients come together. For some it is a sour taste; for others it is a sweet taste. It can be a combination of things rolling across your palate, or a single piece of dark chocolate. For me the perfect bite is a cocktail onion, a piece of sharp cheddar cheese, and a Farman's dill pickle. Just thinking about it makes my mouth water. My senses are heightened and my glands are salivating: the perfect bite.

The psalmist David writes in Psalm 34:8, "Taste and see that the Lord is good! Blessed is the one who takes refuge in Him." The Lord said through David, "Come and get to know Me; come experience My love. Yield your lives and take refuge in My strength. Come and taste Me, experience Me, for I am the perfect bite of life."

This is not about knowledge; it is about learning how to be from God. When we understand His rhythm in life, we discover that we can be fulfilled every day by seeing His will like in the prayer of Jesus, "Your will be done, on earth as it is in heaven." (Matthew 6:10). When we discover this rhythm and this perfect bite, we discover that our mind, heart, body, and soul come into perfect alignment with Him.

Chapter 14

A Deeper Understanding

"Your word is a lamp for my feet, a light on my path" (Psalm 119:105).

When you own a car, you occasionally need to take it in to be serviced. During these visits, the mechanic may ask if you'd like your tires aligned. In older cars there are two adjustments in the front end which help keep the tires parallel to each other and perpendicular to the road. This prevents uneven tire wear and allows for easier maneuverability on the road, especially the curves. You can feel the difference when the front end is in complete alignment. The interesting thing is that you can continue in the direction you want with or without the alignment, but you will do less steering when the tires are properly aligned, and you won't face excessive wear.

In many ways, this is like our spiritual life. We determine which way to go, figure out the best way to get there, and then steer toward our destination. We often rely upon others to help us. We read how-to books or talk to people we consider wise, and if it fits what we're thinking and feeling, we take their advice and follow their lead. Another method we occasionally employ is to pay for the advice of an expert, accepting the advice only when it answers two questions. First, does it make me feel better? Second, does it make sense? These approaches all raise the question, "Is this the right way, or simply a way?"

We can enter into a debate on that question and choose to agree or disagree. Since I am writing about seeking God's rhythm, however, I feel the need to share my thoughts in the hope that through the Spirit of God we can come to an agreement and ensure that we are truly seeking His way, His truth, and His life. This is what alignment is all about. It is not about what I want, when I want it, or how I want it to look. Life is truly about Him and seeking Him. When we achieve this alignment, everything else falls into place.

I recently discovered a television show called ***The Voice*** that's been on for several years. In this show, four judges sit with their backs to the stage and choose singers based not on how they look or perform, but solely on their voices. Listening to these talented people is absolutely amazing. The thing I notice about these singers is that once in a while one goes off key. It is not much, but enough to change the rhythm and nuance of how the song is supposed to sound.

As I have mentioned, I grew up in a church that sang *a cappella*. Before each piece, the song leader would pull out his pitch pipe and blow into it so we could hear the three notes to which we were to tune our voices. It's amazing how you can hear someone singing out of tune when there are no instruments. It is also interesting how you can hear the note in your head, but sing from a whole different place. In many ways, we live life the same way. We read the Word, listen to people, and try to get into alignment with everything that is going on. When we start to live, we find ourselves out of alignment and don't even realize it until the song of life is over or after we have created havoc for ourselves or others.

We can live our entire lives believing our version of truth about God and discover that we were either mistaken in our beliefs or in our interpretations when we die. We can live life the way we think we are supposed to, only to realize later that we are out of alignment. We may even find ourselves heading in the right direction, yet upon our arrival the Lord says, "Why did you work so hard? If only you were aligned with My ways, My truth and My life, you would have gotten here much easier and could have enjoyed the blessings I had prepared for you along the way."

The one thing I want to avoid is writing a how-to book because, to be honest, that is where we begin to fight our battles. As soon as someone gives me advice or wisdom that I do not agree with, I am quick to judge it. I may accept that what they have to say is fine for them, but unless it fits my way of thinking I disregard it. Do you hear in these statements how easy it is to get out of alignment? It is easy to pick and choose what we want to hear, what serves us at the time, and what is the easiest way to get to our destination with least amount of collateral damage.

I needed to understand one key thing in order to stay in alignment and stay away from to focus on what God seeks. This observation had to be brought to the forefront of my heart and mind: *life is not about me.* I have approached this issue from many angles and will continue to show how easy it is to make life about us. We can claim it is about our family, friends, church, work, etc., but the common denominator in each is "me." We have accepted a belief system that makes it sound better when we say, "I am doing this for my family," "I am serving my church," or "I need to do this for my boss." The bottom line is we are choosing this around the basic opinion of "I think" or "I feel" that this is the best way for "me" to live at this time. The art of this subtle supposition is that we believe it is the way we are supposed to live. We flavor life the best we can with God language and doctrinal behavior, living as if this is the way God expects us to live.

Psalm 119 was written about the importance of living, loving, and obeying the Law, the Torah, which are the first five books of the Bible. The reality of that Psalm can be read in terms of the entire Bible, because we find God's truth throughout. I remember teaching a class on the Bible. After studying, I shared how we need to stop looking at the Bible in terms of chapters and verses, Old and New Testaments, and begin looking at the Bible as one book. *The* Book which is the one truth that can guide us to understanding life the way God intended us to understand it—to understand our relationship with Him. It is that relationship that keeps us in alignment—a relationship that He determines for us as our Creator and Lord. With this in mind, as I read Psalm 119 I come away with a greater sense of how I can stay in alignment with the Lord. Let's look at seven verses of this beautiful chapter.

> How can a young person stay on the path of purity? By living according to your word. I seek you with all my heart; do not let me stray from your commands. I have hidden your word in my heart that I might not sin against you. Praise be to you, LORD; teach me your decrees. With my lips I recount all the laws that come from your mouth. I rejoice in following your statutes as one rejoices in great riches. I meditate on your precepts and consider your ways. I delight in your decrees; I will not neglect your word (Psalm 119:9-15).

Within these words we hear the voice of one who truly wants to stay in alignment with God and is far more interested in his relationship with God than all the other nuances of life that can get in the way of this one very special relationship. On this journey, he realized that the way to stay in alignment was by living according to the Word.

Look at these verses in light of John 1:1, "In the beginning was the Word, and the Word was with God, and the Word was God." This profound truth is easily lost when we dissect the Scriptures and hear only what we want to hear. Jesus is the Word. He is the spoken, written, and holy Word. The Bible is about Him, from the beginning of the creation story where He spoke everything into existence, to the final chapters that foretell His return one day to call us home to be with Him and the Father. That book is not for me to tear apart and discover how it best suits my life; it is about Him. The more I read and study it, the more I meditate upon Him in light of what He is saying about Himself. The more I realize who He is, the more clearly I understand who I am, and not the other way around.

The author of this Psalm goes on to say, "I seek you with all my heart" (Psalm 119:10). Alignment is not about me understanding Him with my intellect; it is about me surrendering my heart to Him so that I might truly understand Him and His ways. I do this as the psalmist says so that I might not sin against Him. It is my heart that leads me to live in the unconscious. That place in our being where we live without paying notice to it; it is a behavior or mannerism. That behavior is a natural part of us much like muscle memory in the brain; the positive or negative patterns that we have created play out in our lives whether we are aware of them or not.

If you truly want to know someone, live with them 24/7 for several months. It is then that we can see their lives and their consistency. We can see if their words at church, at work, or in public reflect who they are. This dichotomy exists because we live most of our lives in the unconscious. In public, if we want something or want others to see something, we move into the conscious and live the way we think we ought to. This is not the desire of one who seeks an understanding of God rather than creating God in our own image.

To seek God is to embrace Him in our hearts, to meditate upon His every Word, to talk about Him to others, to have others hold us accountable if the unconscious isn't supporting what we are saying. If we are willing to align our hearts with His passion and His Spirit, our minds will become more aligned with His ways, not our ways.

The final thing I want to share about alignment is best illustrated in Psalm 119:12, "Praise be to you, Lord; teach me your decrees." What this says to me is that it is God who needs to teach us about God. As a society and church, we have taken this attitude when it comes to God: when in doubt, take the easy way out. Let's face it, the easy way in life is to follow the paths of other people, rather than His wisdom, His advice, His leading, and direction.

There are two portions of Scripture that come to mind as I say these words. The first is found in 2 Timothy 2:14-16, in which Paul writes to Timothy,

> Keep reminding God's people of these things. Warn them before God against quarreling about words; it is of no value, and only ruins those who listen. Do your best to present yourself to God as one approved, a worker who does not need to be ashamed and who correctly handles the word of truth. Avoid godless chatter, because those who indulge in it will become more and more ungodly.

Paul is mentoring Timothy in this letter and speaking to him about how to help people deal with false teaching. Note that Paul is not giving his personal advice by saying, "This is how I do things" or "This is how you should do things." He simply instructs Timothy to explain the importance of study, that people might learn what the truth is; Who the truth is; and how He wants us to see, feel, and know Him. That truth is Jesus. That truth is the Word of God. Our task is not to listen to all the pastors and read all the scholarly works we can find in order to help us understand it. These are great resources to help us understand people's opinions, but we should seek Him and His truth, study Him, and meditate on Him. The more we yield our lives to Him and His Word, the more we see and experience life the way He aligns it to be lived.

The second set of verses that come to mind are in 1 John:

> Dear friends, do not believe every spirit, but test the spirits to see whether they are from God, because many false prophets have gone out into the world. This is how you can recognize the Spirit of God: Every spirit that acknowledges that Jesus Christ has come in the flesh is from God, but every spirit that does not acknowledge Jesus is not from God. This is the spirit of the antichrist, which you have heard is coming and even now is already in the world (1 John 4:1-3).

John was writing to the believers about not accepting everything we hear and see just because it sounds or feels good at the moment. Those feelings can lead us astray, causing us to fall out of alignment without ever realizing it. John said not to be afraid to test the Spirits; test what people are saying and believing. If it takes you away from the one truth, the one life, that God calls us to understand and live, then we can easily find ourselves living a life that we want and not the life that He wants.

I have seen dozens of congregations in conflict over many issues, and it happens because they are making life about everything except Him. How can the same Spirit be in conflict? I am in conflict when my head and heart are not aligned, or when my spirit is not aligned with His Spirit. I am not in conflict when He is aligning my head and heart to His truth, His way, and His life. I can live the way I want and still have a chance to get where I want to go, but how much collateral damage am I creating in the process?

What happens if the way I choose is the wrong way? When I am willing to seek first His Kingdom in His way? It may be uncomfortable for a while, but it is only because He is taking the time to realign me so that I am able to see things through His eyes and not my own.

I challenge you to take the time to understand God and get into alignment with His way by seeking God through His understanding and not through your own ideologies. This is another remembrance or stepping stone that helps us along the pathway of truly embracing the God who first embraced us so that we can live the way He designed from the beginning of time. We should live as He told the people of Israel, "I will walk among you and be your God and you will be My people" (Leviticus 26:12), and as Peter reminds us in 1 Peter 2:9, "But you are a chosen people, a royal priesthood, a holy nation, God's special possession, that you may declare the praises of him who called you out of darkness into his wonderful light."

Season 3

From Comfort To Discomfort

Chapter 15
The Cost of the Journey

"Blessed are you when people insult you, persecute you and falsely say all kinds of evil against you because of me" (Matthew 5:11).

How does one remain comfortable in a life of discomfort? That is a rhetorical question because most of us live this way whether we realize it or not. For instance, consider a man who has an addiction and knows it. Part of him wants to change, but not enough to go through the darkness to get there. He remains in that state of discomfort because it is more comfortable than it is to change. Or take the woman who accepts abuse day after day because she doesn't believe in divorce and the cost of standing up for herself is too painful. She continues in that life of discomfort because it is more familiar. Picture the countless people who dislike their job, but remain because it provides a paycheck. They force themselves through each day, eager to get home, continuing to live in discomfort rather than risking the unknown discomfort of a job search or unemployment. Then there is the teenager who follows the opinions and guidance of others, even when he knows what they are doing is wrong. He is willing to live in discomfort because giving in to peer pressure is more comfortable than being without friends.

Oftentimes we choose to live a certain way because the life we really want is too uncomfortable to face. We sacrifice our dreams, our hopes, and sometimes our lives. We do this because it is easier to bear the known discomfort of life and feel comfortable than to choose change, knowing it will be uncomfortable, even though the journey will bring us peace, joy, love, and contentment.

As followers of the Lord Jesus Christ, we do not need to make that choice by ourselves. We have Him. The problem is that we do not listen as closely as we could because we are seeking the comfort of the world—the comfort of our thoughts and ideology. We superimpose God into the picture so we can remain comfortable in times of disillusionment.

The fruit of the Spirit is best understood when we experience them when we are not comfortable in what we are doing, but when we follow the One who is leading. We can discover much about our illusions, misunderstandings, or misled outcomes by seeking clarity around the journey and the rhythm of comfort.

Our customary response to life is to seek comfort. We are willing to do that at any cost. As the story of Exodus unfolds, we discover people who were enslaved under the hand of the Egyptians. It did not start that way. It began with God blessing them through the hand of the Pharaoh by giving them the choice land of Goshen. God blessed them while they were there, and the Scriptures tell us that they grew in numbers and prospered to the point that the Egyptians placed them into slavery out of fear.

The Israelites wanted to be free from the bondage and oppression of the Egyptians, so the Lord sent a leader by the name of Moses. You can read this story in detail in Exodus, but I want to discuss one point that consistently stands out to me. The people were not happy unless they were comfortable, and they would do whatever it took to get comfortable their way rather than God's. *Yahweh* will help us see that life is not about being comfortable with what we have or don't have. It is not about our experiences or lack of experiences, it is about stepping into our greatness with the Lord, embracing the times of discomfort, and finding the truest sense of comfort.

There is a story in Exodus that drives this point home. Along their journey, the Israelites ran out of food and were hungry. How was a leader like Moses going to feed more than three million people in a desert? The people complained and God provided a substance known as manna, or bread from heaven. They were to go out every morning and it would be waiting for them—food for the day—except on Friday when they could gather a double portion, since there would be no manna on the Sabbath day. If the people picked up a double portion on any other day than Friday, the manna would spoil overnight and be full of maggots.

For forty years, God provided food and water for the people. Was that good enough for them? The answer is "no." In Exodus 16 we read that the Lord heard their grumbling and gave them manna. In Numbers 11 we read that manna was no longer good enough; they wanted meat. In Numbers 11:18-20, we read:

> "Tell the people: 'Consecrate yourselves in preparation for tomorrow, when you will eat meat. The Lord heard you when you wailed, 'If only we had meat to eat! We were better off in Egypt!' Now the Lord will give you meat, and you will eat it. You will not eat it for just one day, or two days, or five, ten or twenty days, but for a whole month—until it comes out of your nostrils and you loathe it—because you have rejected the Lord, who is among you, and have wailed before him, saying, 'Why did we ever leave Egypt?'"

There you have it: life as we live it each day. As long as we are comfortable, we will live in any situation and view it as preferable to the alternative. As soon as we find ourselves in a time of discomfort because God is moving, we go back to a place of certainty that we remember as more comfortable. In the long run, we are settling for a greater discomfort because the life we are choosing takes us away from trusting the Lord as provider.

This is not the case in the story of the widow of Zarephath in 1 Kings 17:7-16. It was during a period of great drought that Elijah asked the widow to make him some bread. She only had enough flour and oil to make her son and her one final loaf, and then they would die. Elijah told her to go home and do as he said, first making a loaf for him. He assured the widow that she and her son would have enough oil and flour to sustain them. In that moment the widow had a choice. She could do as the prophet said and step out in total faith and discomfort while risking her own life as well as that of her son. Alternatively, she could choose to ignore the prophet, and out of the comfort of the familiar, make her last loaf of bread and then prolong starvation. Out of her faith in the Lord and charity toward Elijah, the widow complied and was rewarded with sustenance for the rest of her days.

How many of us have chosen to live for the moment—a moment of gratification or pleasure—because it was comfortable? How many of us choose to step into our faith, follow a God we cannot see, and live in that discomfort of faith in the unknown because it is Him we want to follow?

Life is not easy when following the Lord; it requires being uncomfortable. Many writers have described it as times of silence, of challenge; a time when the well is dry, and we feel like we are living alone. All we long for is God to tell us what is next. Sometimes it feels dark, but it is in these times that God's light is shining the brightest, and we can learn to live in the discomfort of our faith and seek Him.

The more we learn about *Yahweh*, the more we are required to live in this state of discomfort; however, it will come with peace and contentment. God's life of discomfort is the greatest place to be because when we feel like it is the farthest, He is the closest. When we feel like He is ignoring us, we realize that He is speaking, but we are not listening. When we feel like He has abandoned us, we realize that He is carrying us.

In order to find the comfort we seek from our relationship with the Lord, we need to understand that our relationship with Him is in the knowing and believing, not in the doing and seeing. *Discomfort* is the tension between taking control and being alone or feeling like we are losing control. In those times, we settle for what we know, what we want, or what we think we want which is our unconscious striving to find that place of comfort, even if it is a familiar discomfort.

As I was writing this, I had a conversation with a woman who had just broken her ankle. The week before, she had set several goals that she was going to accomplish. Being laid up with a broken ankle, however, she was unable to achieve any of them. She told me about some other goals she had set for herself, but had been afraid to pursue them because they would make her too uncomfortable. They were goals about risking more and becoming more vulnerable. She came to an awareness while describing what she did and didn't do, "What I'm realizing is that I am not as in control as I thought, which was an illusion anyway." At that moment she realized what she had just said. Her entire life she had been living on the assumption that she was in control, but realized that all along it was nothing more than an illusion.

We went on to discuss the reason for this illusion. Believing she was in control made her feel comfortable, even though what she was doing and how she was living wasn't what she really wanted. She just didn't want to feel the discomfort of the unknown. The outcome was that she had spent most of her life living in discomfort, consistently accepting the illusion of control that was more comfortable than change—more comfortable than being entirely surrendered to the Lord.

Life isn't about how to escape discomfort; it is actually the opposite. If we want to live an abundant and fulfilled life with Christ, we must learn to embrace discomfort as it is known and accepted as comfort in the heavenlies. It is not about a situation or a feeling, but about a relationship. If you want the relationship with the Lord that He wants you to have, you will be uncomfortable as shown in Isaiah 55:8, "For my thoughts are not your thoughts, neither are your ways my ways, declares the LORD." There are some things that can help us stay in that rhythm where peace and joy abound, even while uncomfortable. One way we can be about the rhythm of God is to stay on the course that He has set for us as believers; we must choose to place our focus and delight on Him and not in what is going to make us more comfortable.

Chapter 16
Stay the Course

"I press on toward the goal to win the prize for which God has called me heavenward in Christ Jesus" (Philippians 3:14).

Being a person who loves to play, sports were an important part of my life. I practically grew up on the baseball diamond. I have had many coaches throughout my life, but the one who stands out above the rest was a coach by the name of Don who helped me realize that playing baseball was as much about mental assessments and reactions as the physical game. This is why every week after fielding and batting practice, we would sit on the bleachers and mentally work through playing a game. Don would give the team a situation and then call out someone's name and have him describe everything he would do during that particular play. It didn't matter whether it was the pitcher, catcher, or right fielder. Everyone had a place to be, and Don made sure that on each play we knew our positions and strategically carried out the play in our minds as if it were a real-life situation. We never lost a game that year, finishing in first place with a 23-0 season.

Just as Don taught me that baseball is as much a mental game as it is a physical one, so it is true in the game of life. Our mental approach is at least as important as physically reacting to the circumstances life brings about. Whether we want to admit it or not, life is lived mainly through the unconscious. How many times have you reacted or acted out and then regretted that you did not do it differently? We call that hindsight. How do we gain foresight in our unconscious? In the mental game of life we can move forward at a steady pace or curl up in bed paralyzed with fear, frustration, depression, or a lousy attitude. The difference between the two outcomes is the mental processes we go through. I have seen both success and disappointment time and again, and it doesn't matter whether you are a Christian or not. If your mindset is not focused on staying the course it was intended to stay on, it will lead to disappointment.

The mental game we play in life happens long before we actually step into the game for the day. Have you seen people who are accomplishing something wonderful, and as you watch them they are so focused on what they are doing that it seems they can't fail? Some people call that moment in the rhythm of life being 'in the zone.' In the movie ***For the Love of the Game,*** you can see this in action as you watch the main character who was focused on a no-hitter which is the highest achievement a pitcher can accomplish in a game. He was so much in the zone that his teammates stayed away from him while he was in the dugout. It was the same for me when my baseball team had a 23-0 season; that was the year I pitched a one-hitter, and it was an amazing day. I was completely focused; it was as if I was one with the ball.

We can make the choice each day to be one with the day and one with God who created the day. It may be a day that everything works out great, even when we are faced with negative events. The difference between one who is in the zone and one who is sitting in the dugout waiting for his time in the big game of life isn't as much about one's ability as it is about his mindset.

In Philippians 2 we read in verses 3-11:

> Do nothing out of selfish ambition or vain conceit. Rather, in humility value others above yourselves, not looking to your own interests but each of you to the interests of the others. In your relationships with one another, have the same mindset as Christ Jesus: Who, being in very nature God, did not consider equality

> with God something to be used to his own advantage; rather, he made himself nothing by taking the very nature of a servant, being made in human likeness. And being found in appearance as a man, he humbled himself by becoming obedient to death- even death on a cross! Therefore God exalted him to the highest place and gave him the name that is above every name, that at the name of Jesus every knee should bow, in heaven and on earth and under the earth, and every tongue acknowledge that Jesus Christ is Lord, to the glory of God the Father.

This is one of my favorite passages in the Scriptures. Paul is talking about being in the Christian zone. It's about having within us a mind not *like* Christ's, but the mind *of* Christ. With the power of the Holy Spirit we can start thinking and feeling as Christ thought and felt. Paul says it a little differently in Romans 12:2 when he writes, "Do not conform to the pattern of this world, but be transformed by the renewing of your mind. Then you will be able to test and approve what God's will is—his good, pleasing and perfect will."

Who doesn't want to know the will of God for their life? We find it when we take on the mind of Christ. I have never seen anyone who has taken on the mind of Christ and found themselves angry, depressed, or even dismayed because things are not turning out the way they planned. If your life is about Christ and about His Father's glory, then you are staying on course with the roadmap He has created for you. It is about being in the zone. We can choose to take on our own mindsets, living according to our own definition of fulfillment, and occasionally experiencing the temporary successes and roadblocks life has to offer. Or we can stay the course of Christ's direction and no matter what happens, experience an abundant and joy-filled life.

It is in the most troubling times or the most uncomfortable situations that we need to have the mind of Christ. The thing that captures my attention the most about the mind of Christ is that no matter what He was doing, how He was feeling, or what was going on around Him, Jesus held to one purpose in life : to glorify His Father. That was the course of His life, and it must be our course if we want to be in the rhythm of life with God.

Staying the course can be one of the most exciting experiences in our lives, or one of the most disappointing if we do not have Christ's mind and heart for the Father.

Pay attention to the different mindsets when you read the stories in Mark 6 and Matthew 14 where Jesus sent out the disciples two by two to do the work of the gospel: heal the sick, cast out demons, and preach the Good News. They came back excited to share with Jesus all that they had accomplished in His name. In response to their great enthusiasm, Jesus wanted to hear what they discovered; however, as they traveled, the multitude followed them and Jesus found Himself spending the next three days preaching to more than 5,000 people which created an opportunity to help others see the heart of the gospel.

The disciples asked Jesus to send the crowd away, but He told them to find something to feed them all. They found five loaves and two fish, and Jesus fed the multitude with them. After the crowd departed, the disciples thought it was their turn to have alone time with Jesus. Instead, Jesus told them to travel by boat to Bethsaida. He then ascended the mountain to pray. When evening came, the waves were rough and the disciples saw a shadow on the sea which they thought was a ghost, but it was Jesus. Peter asked to walk on the water; Jesus said, "Great, come on." As soon as Peter walked on the water, his eyes shifted from Jesus to the waves, and he began to sink. Jesus then gathered Peter out of the water and placed him in the boat; the wind of the seas calmed and everyone was at peace.

Do you hear and see the difference between the mindset of the disciples and the mind of Christ? Christ's life was not about Himself; it was about doing the will of the Father. It was about caring for people, loving them, feeding them, spending time with His Father, and glorifying Him. He was in the zone which was all about His Father. It was about staying the course and not letting anything distract Him from what He set out to accomplish, which ultimately was dying for our sake.

It's not that we're to think like Christ, but to let Christ think for us; to stay on the course of reading His Word while communicating continuously and allowing Him to absorb our minds and hearts. To be in the zone is to have

His beingness and presence in your life, often without realizing, it is His heart and mind that have taken over your spirit. This is the key to life: to glorify the Father in order to get through times of uncertainty, doubt, and confusion while moving from absorption of self to the heart and mind of Christ who humbled Himself for the sake of His Father's will. Being one with Christ is about humility, even when it doesn't make sense to you or feel right at the moment. It is about being prepared, so in a situation like Peter faced, whether it was about needing Jesus' time or having the privilege of walking on water, we walk in God's rhythm and plan for us. It is safe to say that during this time Peter's mind was focused on what he wanted and not on having the mind of Christ.

We see a different Peter in Acts 10 by which time he was willing to stay the course. During the time of the early church before Acts 10, the only way Gentiles could associate with Jews was to become a proselyte and adopt the Jewish faith. It was Peter who baptized the first Gentile, Cornelius, into the Christian faith; Peter was in such a zone that he only wanted to do what was right for the Kingdom. Consequently, he baptized Cornelius' entire household and then went to the Jerusalem council in Acts 11 to defend God's grace. This was a man who held tightly to the mind of Christ. He was a man of conviction, less worried about the opinions of others than in helping someone see the gospel and experience the power of the resurrection. The mind of Christ moved Peter away from the status quo and created a new benchmark resulting in opening the door for all peoples.

Are we willing to be that revolutionary when the Spirit of God is calling us? He is right now! Are you hearing Him? Are we willing to tear down prejudices, theological opinions, and schisms simply because the mind of Christ is compelling us to care for those who are not cared for, or are we more interested in what our future holds than in glorifying the Father?

This is possible because Jesus gave us His heart, His mind, His will, His desire, and His longing for people. Our choice is to determine when we stop seeking comfort and begin finding contentment in Him. We need to learn to live in uncomfortable situations so we can be in the zone and learn to glorify Him each and every moment. This isn't a theory or a dream; it is a reality for all who are willing to believe, accept, and die to self. It is the most uncomfortable comfortable thing we can do. When we live this way, we find contentment; we find it comes with the peace that passes all understanding and it will guard our hearts and minds forever, just like Paul said in Philippians 4:7.

How many pastors and leaders of the church have been willing to put their ministry to question simply because the mind of Christ compels them to? What are you willing to sacrifice to hold dearly to the mind of Christ? Are you willing to shed your old nature for the new? Are you willing to embrace and struggle with the conflict that is within each of us until Christ wins?

Chapter 17
The Conflict Within

"Why do you call me, 'Lord, Lord,' and do not do what I say?" (Luke 6:46).

Words are easy to say, but often difficult to live out. How many times have I asked forgiveness, either mentally or verbally, with the desire and full intent of never doing that again, only to fall once more? Words speak of sincerity, conviction, and promise. They remind me of my desires, my hopes, and my dreams, but words are nothing more than sounds coming out of my mouth if I don't have the determination and fortitude to carry them out.

One phrase that believers use all the time is, "Yes Jesus, I want You as Lord and Savior." We want that peace of knowing we are saved and that God is watching our back. What happens to us when He doesn't do it our way? What happens when we put other gods before Him? When people talk about gods, they are envisioning those false gods that pagans worship—gods made of rock or marble. But have you ever considered that your family could be a god? What about your hobbies, interests, or job? What is a god? A god can be anything we seek or desire more than we seek the Lord Himself. When other things become more important than Him, they become gods.

The issue is not in accepting Christ as Savior. It is not even the acknowledgement of God as God. It is the willingness to yield our lives, our thoughts, our hearts, and our desires to Him so that He is of the utmost importance. This, without a doubt, is a conflict within many believers. At times I see myself believing and feeling that Christ is everything to me; I am so committed to Him that I am willing to do whatever He asks and whatever He wants. That feeling typically lasts a day, maybe longer, but then I fall back to wanting what I want, or I am focused on those things that give me temporary satisfaction. My heart shifts to my wife, family, children, hobbies, and interests. I bring Him with me like I bring a friend. I know He wants me to have those things in my life to enjoy, but if I am honest with myself and with you, I would say that at times all of us love those things more than we love the Lord. That is, until the next time we cry out, "Lord, I want You to be Lord of all."

In the devotional ***My Utmost for His Highest***, in the September 4th entry, Oswald Chambers says it best:

> If anyone comes to Me and does not hate his father and mother, wife and children, brothers and sisters, yes, and his own life also, he cannot be My disciple" (Luke 14:26). He was not saying that this person cannot be good and upright, but that he cannot be someone over whom Jesus can write the word Mine. Any one of the relationships our Lord mentions in this verse can compete with our relationship with Him. I may prefer to belong to my mother, or to my wife, or to myself, but if that is the case, then, Jesus said, "[You] cannot be My disciple." This does not mean that I will not be saved, but it does mean that I cannot be entirely His.
>
> Our Lord makes His disciple His very own possession, becoming responsible for him. ". . . you shall be witnesses to Me . . ." (Acts 1:8). The desire that comes into a disciple is not one of doing anything for Jesus, but of being a perfect delight to Him. The missionary's secret is truly being able to say, "I am His, and He is accomplishing His work and His purposes through me.

These words are written by the Holy Spirit in the heart of a man who captured the essence of what it really means to accept Jesus as Lord. This is the conflict within: we cannot have more than one allegiance. We cannot love the world or the things of the world, even if the Lord expects us to die for our spouse as Christ died for the church. We can neither find nor seek our satisfaction and contentment in anything other than Christ. Once that love has been shown and lived out, we can love others and the things of the world. It is that easy, and it is that difficult.

It is human nature to seek comfort, so we tend to seek the things that bring us the most comfort: job, family, friends, sporting events, and so forth. We spend money on those things that bring us pleasure—a large television, a live concert, a vacation—if it heightens our senses and fills us with joy. Is that wrong? By no means, as long as the Lord has the first place in our thoughts and affections. This is where we come into conflict. For most people, sitting in church, reading the Bible, leading people to the Lord, or attending fellowship gatherings with other believers doesn't bring that same pleasure. In fact, for most of us life would be a constant struggle if not for those relationships and events that bring us joy.

It is in those difficult and uncomfortable times that we can learn just how much God loves us. When we seek Him, we begin to see just how much He loves us, not because He is giving us things, but because we are finding Him. God is having us experience Him in every situation instead of creating a situation to feel God. This is what we do. We create a set of feelings and rationalizations, or even turn to familiar Scriptures, in times of discomfort. We believe that God will rescue us from our despair and create in us the feelings of joy, love, and laughter that we experience in the things of His creation.

My contention is that we are closest to Him when we are in those times of discomfort. In times of comfort we simply do not enter into His rhythm and purpose in order to feel those things He wants us to know and feel. Instead we gravitate toward the things we can control, buy, or be a part of in order to experience that feeling, and we thank God for them. In times like these, are we feeling great joy because we are in God's presence, or because He gave us the desire of our heart for that moment? If the truth be told, it is really those things that we are living for and not the Lord Himself. It is the things that God can produce for us that we seek; it is the comfort of those things that we long for, and not God Himself. Just read about the journey of the Israelites and the struggle the Lord had in getting them to love and trust Him more than water, food, and the things of the world.

The greatest picture of loving God and finding the true essence in difficult times of discomfort is the story of Paul and Silas in the Philippian jail. In Acts 16, we read that Paul and Silas were doing the work of the gospel and were being harassed by a slave girl who was possessed. Out of frustration, he cast out the demon that was inside her which led to Paul and Silas being beaten and thrown into jail. Now that's discomfort! There they were in a grimy jail, locked in shackles with their backsides ripped up and beaten, all because they had cast out a demon. The story goes on to say that at midnight Paul and Silas were worshipping and praising God to the point that the earth started to shake, the shackles fell off, and the prison doors opened. Instead of running for their lives, they used that time to preach to the Philippian jailer who accepted Christ. Amazingly, there was no complaining. In worship they sought God first, before anything they wanted, and found comfort in Him in that time of discomfort.

The same is true with Job, whom we have discussed before. Before Job was blessed twice over, he found comfort in his time of discomfort. He did this not because he was seeking the things of the world anymore, or because he was seeking relief from his sores, but because he sought comfort in the Lord. In that time of discomfort he found comfort, and then he was blessed with the things of the world. This is the difference. We seek the comfort first, in whatever form it takes, before we seek Him. If we do seek Him, it is solely in praying and requesting that He provide for us those things that will bring us comfort. When we get them, we find ourselves thanking Him, but what are we really thankful for—Him or the things that He provided?

Throughout my Christian life I have struggled with one verse more than any other—James 1:2 which says, "Consider it pure joy, my brothers and sisters, whenever you face trials of many kinds." I spent much of my life analyzing and struggling with that verse until I began looking at it from God's perspective rather than mine. I believe God is saying, "You already have the Holy Spirit, so you also have the fruit of the Spirit: love, joy, peace, patience, and the like. With that fruit you are empowered to see and feel My love for you and the world. Within that power of love, you can have joy, not because of the circumstances, but because of who I am. I am who I am. As you go through these trials and tribulations, as you go through this time of discomfort, you can seek comfort in the things of the world or find comfort in Me. The choice is yours. If you embrace the discomfort and seek My face you will be comforted." Thus persecution helps develop and show us the true character of who we are, and who or what we are worshipping. The rhythm of God in times of discomfort may not be easy, but it is in these times that we truly understand who He is and who we are in Him.

As I was thinking about this chapter and struggling with what I wanted to say, the Lord gave me this vision. It was a picture of riding my motorcycle around a sharp curve. The key principle to a successful turn is to stay off your brakes and lean into the curve, keeping your eyes forward. I learned early on that the bike will go where you are looking. Your body adjusts to your eyes, and the more you lean into the curve, the more the bike will be in perfect alignment with the road to consistently ride the curve. Human nature, on the other hand, wants to apply the brake, go around the curve as straight as possible, and look in the direction the bike is pointing. This makes us the most comfortable, but the outcome can be devastating. When you step into the life of feeling uncomfortable you find comfort.

That is the paradox of life. That is the conflict within. We want comfort, but we want it our way, not God's. God may allow us to have that kind of comfort, but at what cost? Like Oswald Chambers says, I may have Him and be saved, but do I really experience the Lord as Lord? The choice is ours. Will He give us what our hearts desire the most? What is in it for you? Are the gifts of God keeping you from experiencing the face of God? How has your life of seeking comfort kept you at an arm's distance from the true comfort and contentment you have been seeking? In times of discomfort, we can fully experience the contentment of our relationship with the Almighty God.

Chapter 18
Golden Contentment

"...for I have learned to be content whatever the circumstances" (Philippians 4:11b).

In the previous chapter, we talked about the struggle that occurs when we experience times of discomfort. As I think about the lives of Job and Paul, my analytical mind wants to take this thought a little deeper for those who cannot live with discomfort. There are people who can tolerate pain and discomfort more, or at least more effectively, than others. It is not that they have a special gene in their DNA, but either consciously or unconsciously, some have learned to live in times of discomfort because they have learned the art of contentment.

I wish I could say that being content in all things was an attribute of mine. I have seen people who have a handle on contentment no matter what the world throws their way. I admire that spirit and cannot wait to attain it. Thus, you see my struggle up front. I want contentment now, and I will not rest until I get it. Of course, I am only playing with the thought that some people long for contentment so much that it makes them uncomfortable to think that they are not content.

The phrase, "I want what I want, when I want it, the way I want it," comes out of a spirit of discontentment. I was a child the first time I saw the ugly monster of discontentment. Oh, how it showed its gnarly face in me each year after Thanksgiving when I would start thinking about Christmas. At the time, Christmas was solely about getting the things I wanted to make me happy and to have a chance to feel important by the gifts I received. In reality, many of us are like this, whether it is a child filled with anticipation at Christmas or a father who comes home expecting dinner on the table and happy kids. Who wants to come home to a nightmare? And mothers, I know you love your children, but if you allow yourself to be honest, there are times that the discomfort of being with them is so great that you seek a place of peace and contentment, if only for an hour.

For many, that spirit of contentment is like an alluring mirage. You see it, but when you try to reach out for it, it seems to move further away with each attempt. In Philippians 4:11 Paul writes, "I am not saying this because I am in need, for I have learned to be content whatever the circumstances." What does that mean? I have been a Christian most of my life and somehow I never felt total contentment in times of discomfort. Then I realized that my contentment was lacking because my focus was on comfort rather than living in discomfort. My emotion—my nature—wanted to take me to the place where I am happy. For many people, being happy is an example of what it means to be content. You have heard the expression, "If Mama ain't happy, ain't nobody happy." Though seen by some as a demeaning saying, it speaks of a reality that is not simply about Mama. It is about every one of us who seeks the things that make us happy or comfortable instead of finding contentment in all areas of our lives, especially in times of discontentment. We have the ability to take our friends and family to a place of unhappiness if they choose to go there with us.

Why are there so many affairs? Why are there so many people going into bankruptcy? Why are there so many commercials promoting things that will make us happy or content? Why do so many people fight the crowds during the holidays just to seek deals so they can show each other how much they saved? Why is it so hard to buy gifts for men? How many fishing lures, guns, golf clubs, or football jerseys does it take to make us content? How many toys do we need to own before we as men say enough is enough? How big does our trailer, camper, or house have to be? How many homes do we "need" to keep up with the Joneses?

What is the real issue? One answer is that we have lost sight of what it means to be content in times of discomfort. We seek the momentary pleasures this world brings us without thinking beyond the moment simply to find contentment. It feels like an alluring drug that we can't get enough of because every time we get into a place of discomfort, contentment goes out the window.

The message our mind seems determined to tell us is, "If you find comfort, you will be content." We keep searching for it without ever finding it, because in reality, contentment shows itself in the uncomfortable times, not in the comfortable ones. This is the paradoxical twist that we see and know as believers, but to the rest of the world it does not match up. How do discomfort and contentment come together?

Listen to the words of the Apostle Paul in his letter to the believers in Corinth who were struggling in their faith,

> Praise be to the God and Father of our Lord Jesus Christ, the Father of compassion and the God of all comfort, who comforts us in all our troubles, so that we can comfort those in any trouble with the comfort we ourselves receive from God. For just as we share abundantly in the sufferings of Christ, so also our comfort abounds through Christ. If we are distressed, it is for your comfort and salvation; if we are comforted, it is for your comfort, which produces in you patient endurance of the same sufferings we suffer. And our hope for you is firm, because we know that just as you share in our sufferings, so also you share in our comfort (2 Corinthians 1:3-7).

It is in our suffering that we find comfort, and it is in our discomfort that we find contentment. Comfort isn't based on the surroundings or the outcome, but in a relationship that moves us from being infected by those surroundings to a place where we can find contentment and peace in our relationship with God.

As we continue to look through the Scriptures, we read in Isaiah 40:1-6:

> Comfort, comfort my people, says your God. Speak tenderly to Jerusalem, and proclaim to her that her hard service has been completed, that her sin has been paid for, that she has received from the LORD's hand double for all her sins. A voice of one calling: "In the wilderness prepare the way for the LORD; make straight in the desert a highway for our God. Every valley shall be raised up, every mountain and hill made low; the rough ground shall become level, the rugged places a plain. And the glory of the LORD will be revealed, and all people will see it together. For the mouth of the LORD has spoken." A voice says, "Cry out." And I said, "What shall I cry?" "All people are like grass and all their faithfulness is like the flowers of the field."

Isaiah is giving us a great picture of a people in exile who are living out the consequences of their sins and who need more than a new place to live, sufficient food, and freedom. They need a Savior; they need a relationship with the God who loves them even in their darkest places. *Yahweh* reminds them that He is there and that they will be treated not as their sins or judgments deserve, but the Great Jehovah is going to give them a place and bring them to a heartfelt relationship with Him. In their darkest times, God is giving them comfort and contentment. It is given even in this uncomfortable place, not because of the things He will give them, but because He has never left them, nor forsaken them as we read in Hebrew 13:5.

In John 16:33 we read, "I have told you these things, so that in me you may have peace. In this world you will have trouble. But take heart! I have overcome the world." This passage was written during one of the most intimate and endearing times with Jesus and the disciples. In John chapters 14-17, Jesus is not only preparing the disciples for His departure in human form, but for an even greater experience with the Lord as they would soon be given the Holy Spirit to dwell within them. He assures them that they will have a place in heaven, live with the power of the Holy Spirit, and live as sons and daughters of the Father—no longer as orphans. What more could they want? Yet they were still uncomfortable with the words of Jesus. In John 14, we read questions that come from the awareness of what is going to happen to Jesus —not what He is giving them. In this discourse we read that Jesus is giving them peace, even when it doesn't make sense to them. They were so concerned about what they would be losing that they lost perspective of what they were hearing and what they were receiving in return.

Every day Jesus is in us to give us peace and contentment, so why do we feel so uncomfortable? Is it because He is not giving us what we want? Is it because it is not coming in a timely manner? Whatever the reason, we must choose to be discontent. We choose to stay uncomfortable in difficult times not because we have not been given peace, contentment, or comfort, but because we are seeking the gold in something other than Him. We are much like the disciples who have lost perspective in what we are hearing and receiving from the Lord in those times of discontentment.

When I am not in a state of peace or contentment, it is not because Christ has left me. It is because I am not choosing to embrace Him at that moment. When I am uncomfortable and discontent, it is not because the Lord is putting the vice to me; it is because I am choosing to no longer seek His face, His way, and His timing.

We make life difficult because we want to create our own paradigm rather than living the one Christ has given us. We convince ourselves that we can live the way we think we should live, with or without Scripture, instead of listening to the voice of God through His Word and His Spirit. Comfort isn't something we create; it is something we receive. The Father, through the Son, has always given it to us. As believers in Jesus Christ we already have love, joy, peace, and patience. Why don't we feel it or experience it? Why do so many people say they will not pray for patience because something bad will happen? We live in a world that walks around seeking the very things we have, and we can choose to accept these things when we receive the God who wants to be known in and through us.

We have contentment when we allow Jesus to live in and through us. We have comfort in times where most people are uncomfortable. If you don't feel it or experience it, then seek His rhythm and feel His heartbeat as you learn to live in His guidance. Trust the Spirit of God; He will never lead you astray.

Chapter 19
Is God Enough?

"But now, this is what the Lord says—he who created you, Jacob, he who formed you, Israel: 'Do not fear, for I have redeemed you; I have summoned you by name; you are mine'" (Isaiah 43:1).

What does it take to truly surrender to the Lord? Is it simply accepting that we are sinners in need of a Savior and then praying for guidance and forgiveness? What makes us saved? Does it come from saying the words and believing that we are not perfect, or does it happen when a person's soul and spirit are awakened to the need within that drives him to the cross for salvation?

When I prayed for salvation, I was at a family camp with my brother and sisters. My mother and stepfather were not saved at that time. The church camp was hundreds of miles from our home, and the pastor and his family took it upon themselves to see that we arrived at the camp. That night, when we were invited to respond, I jumped at the opportunity. I don't remember anything the speaker said, I just knew I wanted to go up and pray.

Was that sufficient to receive eternal life? According to the Scripture and my heart at the time, I would have to say it was. I look back at that moment now and realize that my life took a different course from what I ever imagined it would. Since then I have seen people come to see Christ face to face, and I have helped hundreds of people come to know and deepen their relationship with Him. I am a well-educated man who holds several degrees; however, I have been unfaithful to my wife and family, and I have experienced the loss of friends, respect, ordination, and even membership in a church and denomination that I considered a family. Throughout my life I've felt like I have surrendered everything, only to feel at the same time there is more to give.

I speak of the greatest paradox of all, when your heart and head feel differently at the same time. Even in my darkest time after I confessed my sin and felt the worst I had ever felt, did I truly surrender everything? I thought so, but it is easy to let your life hold on to the things of the world rather than soaking in the love of Christ. We give up what we think we need to give up at the moment, but is that true surrender? How many times do I surrender because I want the Lord to give me a reward? I may even want the very thing I am willing to surrender, or at least communicate that I am surrendering.

What does it actually mean to get lost in Christ? I know what that feels like when I am in worship or experiencing God's power. But what does it mean to really live in that moment—to live wanting to give up more and more simply because you do not want anything to get in the way, but at the same time wanting to live in the abundance of the things God created for your good pleasure?

What is the true hold on people? Is it the things that we are struggling with or the revelation that God is the One who wants sole control of all we have and all that we are? As Christians we get to choose to utilize the gifts He has given us to the fullest so we can experience Him beyond anything we could imagine. This is what Paul might have felt in Philippians 3:8 when he wrote about considering everything as lost for the surpassing greatness of knowing Christ his Lord.

Some might say that surrender looks different to different people. My contention is that it looks different if we focus on the things we are asked to give up. The *act* of surrender is the same for all of us: it is the total relinquishment of allegiance to what we want, when we want, and the way we want it. This is the struggle: the fear of surrender. If I do surrender, will He give me the desires of my heart? At what point can I step in and make His desires real for me? At what point does God honor assertiveness in going after those things in our lives, like our dreams? Can we surrender and go after them at the same time? The overriding question is: are the things or the passions of our dreams more important to us than having a faithful and loving relationship with Him—a relationship in which He is in control of our thoughts and feelings as we pursue those passions and dreams?

I work with a woman who has traveled extensively, but never by herself. She loves to travel and doesn't mind doing it alone, but she chooses to take others so it doesn't feel like she is spending the money on herself. She masked her own value and worth by spending more money. Perhaps she was not enjoying the trips as much as she could have because she did not realize she was worth spending money on. Oftentimes the things are not even the issue, but we make them the issue because we hold on to the lies we believe about ourselves. I challenged her with an exercise; I told her to take a sheet of paper and asked her to write down on one side all the decisions in her life that she had made for herself. On the other side I asked her to write down all the decisions she had made based on the opinions of others. She realized she had more entries on the side of pleasing others than on making decisions for herself. Today, she realizes what a powerful woman she is and recognizes the gifts that God has given her as she steps into that power.

Many years ago I was at the brink of losing everything—my wife, my family, my house, my job, and unbeknownst to me at the time, my friends. Everything I had lived for nearly vanished because I was trying to hold on to my way of thinking and feeling and justifying my actions accordingly. It happened one day that I found myself confessing to being unfaithful to my wife, my family, my ordination, and my commitment to the church. For the next several months I found myself in deep remorse, depression, shame, and guilt. I found solace in my Bible, my therapist, my books, and my Yorkshire terrier, Maggie, who took many walks with me as I prayed and sought what the Lord desired me to see.

One day, as I was lying in bed, which I found to be my most secure place, I was reading a book by Henri Nouwen titled ***The Return of the Prodigal Son***. In that book, Nouwen writes that at different times in our lives we can relate to being the younger son, the father, or the elder son. I was intrigued. I started to read his rendition of one of the most beautiful passages of Scripture from Luke 15. In his book Nouwen recorded how the son was walking back from working with the pig farmer and was willing to do anything to be back in his father's household, even if it meant being a servant. As he was thinking about what he was going to say, he saw his father at a distance running to him. Before the son could say anything, he heard the words from his father, "My son, the beloved." At that moment I cried. I cried so profusely that I could not stop. Hearing those words when I felt totally abandoned changed my perspective and provided the hope and healing I needed at that moment. The writer of Luke records Jesus saying it this way,

> "When he came to his senses, he said, 'How many of my father's hired servants have food to spare, and here I am starving to death! I will set out and go back to my father and say to him: Father, I have sinned against heaven and against you. I am no longer worthy to be called your son; make me like one of your hired servants.' So he got up and went to his father. But while he was still a long way off, his father saw him and was filled with compassion for him; he ran to his son, threw his arms around him and kissed him" (Luke 15:17-20).

To be kissed by the father is the greatest feeling one can ever imagine. It was on my daily walk that I verbally spoke the words, "I am no longer a servant, but a son." For the first time I allowed myself to feel like a son. I had spent my entire life serving others, striving to meet their needs, and serving the Lord. I was trying to be a good pastor while at the same time serving my family by trying to be a good father and husband. The truth be told, I did not succeed in my expectations. Now I got to simply be a son and live for Him, whatever that meant.

Since then, I have worked to pick up the pieces, recapture my dream, make a difference in the Kingdom the best I can, and love my children and my wife of over three decades. My world doesn't look like I once pictured it, even thinking that God was going to restore me a certain way. What I wanted was good fortune and the ability to make a huge difference in the world. That still might happen, but it doesn't really matter in the long run. In the subsequent years, I have found myself dealing with doubt about myself, confusion about today, and discomfort about God's plan. I'm living uprightly and honestly before God and my family, but I'm not sure where the Lord is going to take me because I do not have a clear picture of tomorrow. The difference about going through things like this now is that I am clinging to my deeper relationship with God as my Father and me as His son-that's what matters in the long run.

When I shared the beginning of this chapter with my friend and editor, she gave me some great advice: "Go back to where you were those years ago. What would life look like if you lost everything?" I said, "I already know what that feels like." She then asked the golden question, "What is God saying to you?" I heard the words coming out of my heart, "You are enough!!!" Then it hit me. Surrender is not as much about giving up something as it is about receiving God's full assurance that I am enough and I am His beloved. As humans we feel the need to prove ourselves by our acts of service, thoughts, education, and wealth. God doesn't necessarily want us to give up those things unless they are serving as a god, but what He is asking us to believe is that we are enough without them. It doesn't matter what we do or how we do it. He wants us to know that we are enough.

Let's take a minute and look at the elder son in the story as well. He was angry because of how the father was treating the younger son who had squandered his inheritance. Luke 15 continues:

> "The older brother became angry and refused to go in. So his father went out and pleaded with him. But he answered his father, 'Look! All these years I've been slaving for you and never disobeyed your orders. Yet you never gave me even a young goat so I could celebrate with my friends. But when this son of yours who has squandered your property with prostitutes comes home, you kill the fattened calf for him!' 'My son,' the father said, 'you

> are always with me, and everything I have is yours. But we had to celebrate and be glad, because this brother of yours was dead and is alive again; he was lost and is found'" (Luke 15:28-32).

What was the elder son feeling at the time? My thought is that he was envious because he was the one dealing with the fallout of the younger son. He was the faithful one; he was the one who had submitted to the will of the father, but he did not know how he felt about that until the younger son came home. At that moment, his true feelings about his service were revealed. He too lost perspective that he was enough. The father said, "Everything I have is yours." What more did he need from the father that had not already been given him? It was the elder son who needed to feel like he was enough.

Until we realize that we are enough, we will never be able to hold the tension and hear the heartbeat of God. We will hear the rhythm we think it is beating, and we may be close. We will read about what He wants in His Word and be obedient like the elder son, but will we truly hear what He is saying to us and the world? The rhythm of God is about surrendering to His desire, His way, and His will, and it starts by realizing that we are enough. When that happens, everything we are doing, seeing, and experiencing falls into His rhythm. Only then can we see what is truly important: how He can make a difference in our lives and in the lives of others.

Surrender comes in a simple and powerful three-word phrase, "I AM ENOUGH." Those three words will either haunt us for the rest of our lives or set us free to serve Him with all our heart, soul, mind, and body. Jesus has set us free from our sins. That is the glory of the Good News, and with that news the door opens for us to see, feel, and experience that we are enough. Not because of who we are or what we do, but simply because we are!

This is the great and true paradox. We see, feel, and experience surrender as our need to give up something, not the art or gift of receiving. The more I allow myself to receive the fact that I am enough, that I need nothing else but my relationship with God, the easier it is to let go of the very things I do not want to give up—those things that I believe make me a self-sufficient man, a great leader, or a beloved father. So instead of letting go, we hold on until we get something better to replace it.

Having open hands and an open heart is about knowing, seeing, and feeling that in the eyes and heart of God we are enough with Him. Paul illustrated this in Philippians 4:13 when he said, "I can do all this through him who gives me strength." These powerful words come from a man who found comfort in the most uncomfortable times and discovered this truth which is yet another stepping stone of life. A foundational stone which reminds us that God is enough as we realize we do not need the things of this world for peace, joy, and love; all we need for a fulfilled life is God Himself because He is sufficient in all things. How many of us quote Philippians 4:13 but cannot receive the things that the Lord wants to give us because we are clinging to the very things that we think will bring us comfort? We must find comfort in Him and in Him alone because we are enough, just as He is enough.

Season 4

From Independence

To Dependence

Chapter 20

Not by Power or Might

"So he said to me, 'This is the word of the LORD to Zerubbabel: Not by might, nor by power, but by my Spirit,' says the LORD Almighty" (Zechariah 4:6).

There is nothing like the sound of a muscle car. The rev of the engine as the body rises up and starts to vibrate, all eight cylinders firing in synchronicity; it is music to a car lover's ears. There is such power in the old muscle cars. When I was in college I had a van that was converted and painted different shades of purple; it was one of a kind. A friend of mine wanted to trade cars for a day so he took my van, and I took his forest green Plymouth Roadrunner. All you had to do was put your foot on the accelerator and his car would leave a little rubber on the road. That day I was driving through the campus when I hit the accelerator and the tires started spinning, and unbeknownst to me, the owner of the car was watching. That was the only time I drove his car, but it was fun while it lasted.

There is something about power, whether it is stepping on the accelerator of a muscle car or stepping into a position of leadership or control. Power can be detrimental to those who are following your lead, or you could be the hero. To me, one of greatest presidents in the United States was Harry S. Truman. I was not around when he was president, but he had to make some of the most difficult decisions, like dropping the atomic bomb. What a monumental decision that was. Some people saw him as a hero—others as a murderer. I am sure there is not a president alive who would want to make that kind of decision. Like with President Truman, every major decision a president makes has the possibility of tremendous consequences. The same is true for governors who have the ability to pardon convicted criminals or police officers who have to decide whether or not to draw their guns.

Power comes in many different forms, and countless decisions are made each day by those in positions of power. It may be a parent who won't allow a child to stay at a friend's house, or a five-star general deciding which troops will be left in a foreign country and which will get to go home. The situations may seem different, but they are simply variations of the same power. Some decisions affect thousands or millions of people; other decisions affect only one or two. It doesn't matter, it is all the same power. Some decisions affect a person for the good, while others destroy an entire city. Whenever we make a decision, whether it is for ourselves or for others, it comes when we are willing to step into a position of power. It takes the same power to decide to walk away from a situation or to stay and fight. To remain passive or become aggressive, to act or react; the impact or the effects may be different, but it is the same power that allows us to make those decisions.

Some people live for power, while others are willing to relinquish their power. In either case, whether we realize it or not, we are still exerting power. When Christ allowed the Roman government to take Him captive and crucify Him, wasn't He displaying power? Some of the most wise and powerful people do not say much, but when they speak, people listen. Some of the most dangerous people are those who say one thing, but think and act differently. Power can be manifested in many different forms; it can be both deceiving and alluring at the same time.

As believers, we say Christ is Lord and Savior and that He has the power, but how often do we say one thing and then do the opposite? How many of us say we are going to wait and trust His timing, but out of anxiety or lack of patience we strive to take control? How many times have you tried to fix a problem within a congregation, only to make things worse? How many times have you prayed for someone and believed that God was going to heal them, but they have not stepped into the power of His healing?

During the time of Haggai and Malachi, the prophet Zechariah was known as the prophet who offered hope, restoration, and the destruction of Israel's enemies. In one of his well-known verses in chapter four, he writes to the people of Israel on the reestablishing of the nation saying, "So he said to me, 'This is the word of the LORD to Zerubbabel: Not by might, nor by power, but by my Spirit, says the LORD Almighty.'"

If you look at the book of Ezra, you read how a remnant went back to Jerusalem during the time of King Artaxerxes to rebuild the temple. Out of fear for the power once displayed by the people of Israel, he grew concerned, and so the building of the temple ceased until the time of King Darius. It was Zechariah who pointed out that the temple would not be built by the hand of man, but by the power of the Spirit. God's power is often seen by man as the power of man. Unless it is a supernatural miracle, it is difficult to recognize on a day-to-day basis who is doing the work. Is it the hand of God or the hand of man? It may look the same in the beginning, but with time and results we can clearly see the hand of God.

So how do we understand and embrace the power of God effectively? It is in that great paradoxical moment that we can see His hand. Those are our moments of surrender—times that we are willing to be completely dependent on Him. Surrender doesn't always look the way we think it should. It doesn't mean that we simply give up and sit on the sidelines, letting God do all the work. God chose to use the people of Israel to reflect His power to the world. He is waiting for us to surrender to Him so we can be His light in this dark world. So what does *dependence* mean? It is defined in three simple, yet powerful words: *reflect, resign, and restore.* These words capture the essence of dependence. In the eyes of man they are merely words, but in the hands of God they reflect power like none can create on their own.

Think Before You Act

Too often destructive power occurs when people act before they think. We are prone to act or react to what is going on. Part of the reason is that humans have an innate sense of self-preservation. This means that we are driven to survive and want what we want, when we want it, and the way we want it. If things don't look the way we think they ought to look, or feel the way we want them to feel, we tend to react first and then engage our minds later. At times that can be good, but in other ways we can become disruptive to what God has in store. Take, for example, the impetuous Peter, who in Matthew 14 saw Jesus walking on the water and immediately wanted to join Him there. Jesus invited him to come , and Peter got out of the boat and walked until his intellect kicked in. It was when he took his eyes off Jesus that he started to drown.

During the exodus from Egypt, time and again we read that when the people of Israel were not getting what they wanted, they complained, saying repeatedly, "You brought us to the desert to die." Why would the Lord create ten miracles in Egypt, followed by the parting of the Red Sea, water spouting from a rock, and manna falling from heaven simply to let them die in the desert? In both situations they have the same thing in common. They immediately began to react instead of reflect.

Reflection does not take a long time. It can be as easy as inviting God into the moment and yielding our hearts to Him. When we take the time to reflect on Him, we can fully assimilate Him. As believers, when we reflect on His image we become one with Him. Jesus Himself said in John 14:9b, when asked to reveal the Father to the disciples, "Anyone who has seen me has seen the Father." Even though we are not God, we can show His image, power, and holy presence. If Peter had reflected on Christ's power, would he have stayed afloat? What would have been the result if the people of the exodus had reflected on the power, protection, and majesty of God? Their trip might not have taken 40 years. They stayed in the wilderness due to a rebellious spirit, not a reflective spirit. The more I reflect on His power, His majesty—what He has done, is doing and will do—the more I move away in the unconscious from the desire to do things my way and move toward depending on Him for everything.

Isn't this what He desires from us? Not to depend on our own strength, but to use our strength and give it to Him so that we might mimic the words of songwriter Andre Crouch, who once sang, "All that I am or ever hope to be, I owe it all to thee, to God be the glory." We live in an illusion if we think for a minute that God needs us in a position of power to accomplish His will and His way. If we believe that, we should read the story of Balaam and his talking donkey in Numbers 22. It would benefit us to realize that God does not need us; He wants us, and He wants dependent hearts that are willing to reflect on His promise, power, and passion. When we take time to reflect, we find that we are in the rhythm of dependence. When we close the door to what the Lord wants and try to force things our way, we are moving in the direction of independence to maintain control. Then we couch our words and actions with God talk in hopes that others will not see the wolf in sheep's clothing.

As we reflect, we can choose to resign, to yield our way to God's way, our will to His will, our habits to His habits; believe me, our way will not look the same as His. The greatest illustration of this comes from the battle between the Israelites and the Amalekites in Exodus 17. The people were shepherds, not fighters. They knew how to protect themselves from the beasts of the field, not against the swords and spears of mankind. Nevertheless, the people went to battle. The Scripture says that Moses, Hur, and Aaron went to the hillside, and as long as Moses held the rod up in the air, the Hebrews were victorious. As soon as his hands lowered, the Amalekites would gain the advantage. Moses reached a point that he could no longer hold his tired arms in the air, so Aaron took one arm and Hur the other, holding them up until the battle was over.

Talk about resigning to the will of the Lord! The battle had nothing to do with how well the people fought, but how dependent the win was on the leader who held his hands in the air and experienced the almighty power of God. Surrendering to God meant they still had to fight. The battle was not theirs to win, only to participate in, for the battle belonged to the Lord and the cooperation of the leadership. In today's congregations, we have powerful and influential leaders, but how many of them are running the church with their arms in the air, dependent upon the Lord and others to help them win the battle?

This doesn't mean we sit back as Christians and simply surrender to what is going on around us as we act. Are we acting in the power of God with our arms and hearts directed to Him or are we acting independently with the desires of what we want and then adding God into the equation so it looks better than it is? Congregations are dying and conflicts are occurring not because we are dependent on the Lord, but because we are reacting independently and bringing God into the equation after we have laid our plans and started to live them.

Once we reflect and resign, we have the Spirit of Christ to restore us. God is not in the business of building new, but in restoring, which seems like an oxymoronic statement today. Look around and you find a new church being built on almost every block. Each congregation has its own little niche to promote. They all seem to say they are Bible-oriented, but they have a unique way of showing their understanding of the Bible. We build these congregations to attract people who need the Lord, but often find the church filled with those who are disgruntled from their last place of worship, or who come looking for the next new thing to hold their interest. Is that really what the great commission is all about? If you look in Genesis 1 and 2, you will read that God had already built the perfect world. After each thing He created, whether it was the birds of the air, the fish in the sea, or mankind, God said, "It was good."

From that point on, mankind could not improve on what God had done, and ever since Adam and Eve ate of the fruit, the Lord has desired restoration. Why did the Lord come Himself? The Scripture says to redeem us, reclaim us, and to restore us to a right relationship with Him. Wasn't that the Lord's intent for the people of Israel? He built the city; He built the temple, and because of their disobedience and their propensity toward independent thinking, what God built was destroyed. After 40 years in exile, God called men like Ezra, Nehemiah, and thousands of others not to build, but to restore; to bring the people back to a place of honoring and worshipping the Lord.

Somehow we feel like it is our business to usurp His power and build the right fellowship, the right relationship, or the right gathering. When I look at the Scriptures I don't see God telling us to build the perfect building or bring in the right people. I see the Scripture telling us to feed the hungry, clothe the naked, and visit the imprisoned. This is all about restoration; a people that yields or resigns their lives to Him, people who are not building, but restoring.

Take a look at Jesus and the Samaritan woman in John 4. Here was a woman who had five husbands, and the man she was living with at that point was not even her husband. This story is all about restoration—the restoring of a woman and a nation that felt ostracized. It is a story about a woman who had to surrender her way of thinking and feeling in order to find true and total restoration. She became one of the most influential women in the Bible, not because she read the great leadership books of her time, but because she was willing to surrender her thoughts to His thoughts, her ways to His ways, and her will to His will. This is where the power lies.

Throughout the centuries we have spent our lives trying to build something instead of restoring people back to Him. The more we rely on our independent mindset and power through performance, the more we want to build and the more we are simply building on sinking sand. The more we reflect, resign, and restore, the greater our chance to experience heaven on earth. And isn't that His desire? I am not putting down powerful leadership, but the most powerful people are those who have learned to reflect, resign, and restore; they have learned the secret of God's power. It is in these times of reflecting, resigning, and restoring that we move from our ways to His ways, from our thoughts to His thoughts, and from our will to His will.

Chapter 21

Not My Will

"My Father, if it is not possible for this cup to be taken away unless I drink it, may your will be done" (Matthew 26:42b).

Have you ever heard or said, "Things simply did not turn out the way I expected or wanted them to?" This phrase speaks so much truth in my life. I am known as a planner; as I've said before, I plan spontaneity. I have been working on being more spontaneous in my life, letting go and not worrying about the outcome, but it has taken me half a lifetime to get here. I hope it will not take as long to become even more spontaneous than I am now. Being one who analyzes almost everything I do, I enter a moment expecting to move toward my desired outcome. When I see that the outcome might look different, my stress level increases because I feel like my plan, my predetermined outcome was the right one. Those who are spontaneous also have an idea of how an event will look. They simply do not know what it is until the event or the situation is over. If it wasn't as fun or as interesting as they thought it would be, we can see the disappointment come over their being.

Whether we want to admit it or not, we are selfish people. We seek whatever makes us the happiest, or at least we seek a favored outcome for ourselves and those we love. When that doesn't happen, we often react by trying to control the events as best we can for the most favorable outcome possible. Total dependence may be in our vocabulary, but we are only dependent to the extent that it favors us at that moment. Human nature breeds independence. We want to see things a certain way and we want the outcome to lean toward favoring what we want. That has been our battle with the Lord ever since the garden. Adam and Eve wanted to know what it was like to experience the fruit that came from the Tree of Knowledge of Good and Evil. They chose not to leave things just as God wanted them to be.

You can see this same kind of behavior in James and John, Jesus' devoted disciples, in Mark 10:35-41:

> Then James and John, the sons of Zebedee, came to him. "Teacher," they said, "we want you to do for us whatever we ask" "What do you want me to do for you?" he asked. They replied, "Let one of us sit at your right and the other at your left in your glory." "You don't know what you are asking," Jesus said. "Can you drink the cup I drink or be baptized with the baptism I am baptized with?" "We can," they answered. Jesus said to them, "You will drink the cup I drink and be baptized with the baptism I am baptized with, but to sit at my right or left is not for me to grant. These places belong to those for whom they have been prepared." When the ten heard about this, they became indignant with James and John. Jesus called them together and said, "You know that those who are regarded as rulers of the Gentiles lord it over them, and their high officials exercise authority over them. Not so with you. Instead, whoever wants to become great among you must be your servant, and whoever wants to be first must be slave of all. For even the Son of Man did not come to be served, but to serve, and to give his life as a ransom for many."

Here we have two people who have been following the ways of the Lord, observing His heart as a servant, basking in His words, and they are special as His disciples. With all they were watching, experiencing, and breathing in, they still wanted more. They wanted one to sit on the right and one to sit on the left in Christ's Kingdom which would give them positions of value, honor, respect, and authority. They wanted to be His right-hand and left-hand men. They thought they were ready, and they may have even thought they deserved those positions.

They were living what I call the "independently dependent" life. They wanted to be servants of Jesus; they wanted to be devoted to Him; they wanted to be on the forefront of the battle, but they wanted to do it in a way that made sense to them. Isn't that the way many believers want to live today? We want to be truly serving Him; we are willing to say, "Yes, Lord, I will follow You wherever You go. I will be with You whatever You want to accomplish as long as we do it my way." We may not be consciously saying these words like James and John, but how many of us come to prayer not with desires, but expectations? Then, if the Lord does not answer just the way we want, we tend to question Him. Some even go after it without His power.

I believe James and John had the deepest sincerity, yet in their own minds they wanted what they wanted. Jesus even challenged them with the question, "Are you willing to drink the cup that I am drinking?" They said yes, and in their minds they were willing to do whatever it took. But then in Matthew 26 we read of their devotion to their own will rather than the will of the Father. Let's look at the words of Matthew as we come together in one of the most powerful passages the Scripture offers us. After Jesus had just washed their feet and drunk of the cup with His disciples, we read:

> Then Jesus went with his disciples to a place called Gethsemane, and he said to them, "Sit here while I go over there and pray." He took Peter and the two sons of Zebedee along with him, and he began to be sorrowful and troubled. Then he said to them, "My soul is overwhelmed with sorrow to the point of death. Stay here and keep watch with me." Going a little farther, he fell with his face to the ground and prayed, "My Father, if it is possible, may this cup be taken from me. Yet not as I will, but as you will." Then he returned to his disciples and found them sleeping. "Couldn't you men keep watch with me for one hour?" he asked Peter. "Watch and pray so that you will not fall into temptation. The spirit is willing, but the flesh is weak." He went away a

> second time and prayed, "My Father, if it is not possible for this cup to be taken away unless I drink it, may your will be done." When he came back, he again found them sleeping, because their eyes were heavy. So he left them and went away once more and prayed the third time, saying the same thing. Then he returned to the disciples and said to them, "Are you still sleeping and resting? Look, the hour has come, and the Son of Man is delivered into the hands of sinners. Rise! Let us go! Here comes my betrayer!" (Matthew 26:36-46).

Let's take a moment to reflect upon the actions of Peter, James, and John. They were the ones who went a little closer to the place where Jesus prayed; they were the three who were on the Mount for the great transfiguration. They experienced Jesus differently from the other disciples, and James and John were the ones who wanted to sit by His side. Yet, instead of honoring Jesus and staying awake, they fell asleep because they were tired. Oh how easy it is to see things through our own lenses. From James' and John's points of view it may or may not have been alright to fall asleep, but they did it anyway. Can you imagine a battle in which a general looks around and sees his two right-hand people asleep? I am sure they would not hold their respective positions for long.

Here we have two top officials in the movement that the Lord put into place and they are sound asleep. They were as independently dependent as they possibly could be. What was Jesus doing at this time? He was aligning His heart with the heart of the Father. He was disengaging from a mindset that could breed independence to one of total dependence. **One of the greatest truths I have come to realize is that the battle over sin was not fought on the cross, it was demonstrated in the garden.** The battles of independence and wayward thinking were fought right there at that time.

As we look at Jesus in the garden, the **first** thing we see is that it is alright to examine your feelings and acknowledge them for what they are. Until we do that, we cannot truly come to grips with what we believe, feel, and think. Jesus showed us His desire when He prayed, "Father let this cup pass from me." He knew what He was going to face. He knew the pain of separation from the Father—the ridicule, the torture, the struggle for His disciples as they would watch their leader being dragged away. He knew the anger and vengeance on the part of the religious rulers as they mocked and beat Him. They subjected Him to an intensity of suffering that would compel most people to resort to self-survival; it is a place where independence finds its energy and people are willing to say or do anything to be set free from the discomfort they are currently feeling.

Jesus tells us His human desire: to have the cup taken away—to find another way so He would not have to endure the hardship He was about to face. In that moment of recognition, He said, "Yet, not my will but Yours be done." That is complete dependence.

At this time in His life, Jesus was resolvedly surrendering to the will of His Father, to the very will that He was sent to Earth to fulfill. Although it was what He wanted, He also wished it could be done differently from the way it was about to happen. These thoughts were so difficult to bear, and His experience was so passionate that He sweat drops of blood. I can't begin to imagine what He was experiencing for this to occur. And while He was feeling this, what were His right-hand men doing? They thought they were dependent and surrendered, but were they? Jesus shows us true dependence; He was willing to lay it on the line no matter what. As difficult as it appears in the Scriptures, it was worth it to Him to accomplish the will of the Father rather than let any of His human thoughts and feelings get in the way.

The **second** thing we come to realize in this passage is that we have a choice. We can say we are dependent, that we are surrendered, but when the pressure is on we have a choice to let the will of God unfold without our knowing the outcome or to fight it and come as close as we can and still hold on to our independence. Dependence on the Father is unadulterated abandonment. It is hard to imagine what that looks like until we come face to face with it—when we have the opportunity to pray, "Father let this cup pass from me, if not, let Your will be done." These pivotal moments can come in the blink of an eye, or they can brew until we choose to release our will to our current situation.

Jesus shows us that we do not have to be passive and just let things happen. Jesus was not passive in the garden; He was not just sitting and waiting to die on the cross. He was praying and exhorting. He was yielding, teaching, loving, and surrendering throughout the evening. Jesus was tempted to throw it away and be the powerful ruler on earth, as His disciples and followers wanted. Even though it was a choice for Jesus, the decision was made when He came to do the will of the Father, which was evident as He stepped confidently out to greet His betrayer.

It was not His will that He wanted to accomplish, but the will of the Father. Whenever our minds and hearts lean toward our feelings or thoughts, we make our choice that much harder. But when our hearts, thoughts, and actions are pointed to the Father, as difficult as the decision is, the choice is easier. No matter what we are thinking, or trying to put into place when trials and tribulations come our way, we do not and will never know the outcome. Jesus is showing us the only way through those trials and tribulations. We must choose to take our eyes off what we want, when we want it, and how we want it; embrace the heart of the Father in total abandonment; and let Him accomplish His will—His way, in our lives. That is dependence.

The **third** and final thing we see in this story is that dependence is possible. Jesus agonizes over this moment. He is praying and sweating drops of blood. He is worn out and alone, with the exception of His relationship with His Father, the only relationship that matters. Where are His disciples, His followers, His devoted ones? They are sleeping.

Jesus could have chosen to simply say, "I give up; this is it. If even my most devoted disciples do not get what I am doing and cannot stay awake and prepare for just one hour, why bother?" Have you ever given up because in your mind and heart you have felt entirely alone? Have you ever been so frustrated with life that you think, why bother? Those are true and valid feelings, but so often they come about because we have our eyes and heart focused on the feelings of the people around us instead of on the Lord.

We cannot look at what other people are thinking, feeling, and even perceiving around us and become dependent on Lord. We can see it and acknowledge it, but if we want to be in a deep spiritual relationship, our eyes and heart need to stay on the Lord and not on the actions or reactions of others. The more we focus on what people think and feel, including ourselves, the more we are subject to be that independently dependent person. The more we seek, acknowledge, and go back to the face of Jesus Himself, the more we can come to that place of surrendered dependence.

After He spoke with His disciples, Jesus did exactly that. He went back to prayer, back to focusing and seeking to fulfill the will of His Father. Jesus was not only showing this ability, but remember in John 16 He said to His disciples, "I must go so you can have My Spirit in you." Wow! We have His Spirit and with that Spirit comes the same ability to surrender—the same mindset to cry out, "Lord, I don't want to experience what I am experiencing, let this cup pass from me." We can cry out these words with all the heart and passion with which we were created. We also have the power within us to say, "Let not my will be done, but Yours" and then surrender to the outcome however it unfolds, with the only expectation and desire being that the Father is glorified in all that we are experiencing at that moment.

We have the same Spirit that was in Christ, all we get to do is let go and be dependent on God, even in the most uncontrollable circumstances. Our greatness—our beingness comes out when we learn how to be who we are in that great state of dependence.

When Jesus left the garden He said to His disciples, "Rise. Let us go!!!" He was resolved and empowered. He was ready to take on the cross, the people, the opposition, and the full heavenly authority was with Him every step of the way. He had no questions, no doubts, no fears, and no regrets. He was in such a place of dependence that He was willing and ready to let the events unfold throughout the next morning until He uttered His final words, "It is finished." This is absolute dependence. He not only showed us the way, the truth, and the life, but fulfilled His Word in John 16 by giving us that same Spirit and power that led Him to the cross and on to victory while giving His Father the glory through it all.

We have that opportunity to be dependent and powerful at the same time. The power Jesus felt did not come out of His struggle, His ability to heal, or His capacity to call down fire and brimstone from Heaven. His power came in His ability to be dependent as He sought the will and presence of the Father in such a way that He could face the most difficult time in His life with consummate resolve.

This is ours for the choosing. Do you want to live a life in which you have one foot in the world of independence and one foot in the heavenly realm, saying you want to do the will of the Father? Or are you truly willing to relinquish your will and your way to the One who has the ability to lead you to your own cross each and every day? The glory and power of the garden is ours for the taking. Are you willing to step into it as you pray, "Let not my will be done, but Yours?" How can we experience abundant life like this each and every day?

In the next two chapters we will explore the importance of leaning and abiding as the mainstays that will keep us moving in a forward rhythm with Him as we depend more on Him and less on ourselves.

Chapter 22
Leaning on the Promises

"For no matter how many promises God has made, they are 'Yes' in Christ. And so through him the 'Amen' is spoken by us to the glory of God" (2 Corinthians 1:20).

Each day we can say the words, "Let your will be done." If you're like me, when you say that prayer you are facing your cross or burden, but that burden stays with you day in and day out. It is not a momentary presence. It can be with you for a year or two, or even for a lifetime. How can we hold on to that same faith, that same love, devotion, and commitment day in and day out when the trials and tribulations in our life go on in perpetuity? What happens if we become like the Apostle Paul who prayed for healing, yet the Lord never healed him the way he wanted? What happens to those who are burdened by fear for a lifetime? How can they maintain that level of dependence until the day the Lord calls them home? How do we fight the constant battle of seeking what we believe is an abundant life and finding ourselves in the garden praying for this cup to pass quickly?

Promises of a Good God

It is important for us to realize that the Lord not only gives us the garden experience with His Spirit, His power, mind, and heart, but also His promises. Throughout my life, I've discovered that when I am struggling, fearful, and anxious about an outcome, I find comfort in the words, "I promise." Oftentimes, I have put a lot of trust and hope into people's promises, only to be disappointed. Nevertheless, my heart seems to yearn for those words time and again, "I promise." One of the greatest joys a person can experience is to lean on someone's promise and then see that promise fulfilled. What a delightful and incredible experience!

As we grow increasingly dependent on God, each day we can choose to either lean on His promises or tell Him we do not trust His Word in the same way we don't trust the promises of others. When this happens, what I see us doing is moving God to our realm of thinking and logic instead of seeing Him from His perspective with the help of the Holy Spirit.

I once had a conversation with another believer who openly and honestly admitted that the thing he struggles with most is seeing innocent children suffering and dying daily, and trying to align that with a loving and compassionate God. From the human standpoint, I cannot agree with him more. Those two things in my mind create a paradox. How can we rationalize seeing God as loving and compassionate when He allows these bad things to take the lives of so many innocents? How does it make sense? What about nations in which the populace faces hunger and contaminated water on a daily basis resulting in death and untold suffering? What about the children of the world who are born with AIDS?

We can look at all these things and find an endless supply of fuel to feed the fires of brokenness, discontentment, and independence. We try to take matters into our own hands simply because we think or feel that God is doing nothing about all of the pain and suffering going on around us, including our own. Just how can I be completely dependent and endure this kind of hardship? Again, dependence is a revelation of choice. We can do our best to make a difference; to live a life that is wholesome, pleasing, and honoring as we move toward social consciousness and change. But what if we find ourselves disappointed repeatedly because we are trying to do these things from our own strength and power with the hope that we will get the results we are seeking? This line of thinking can lead us to perceive God's acts and motives as if He were finite.

Once again we return to Isaiah, who reminds us that God's thoughts are not our thoughts and that His ways are not our ways. Using human logic on God, will not allow us to comprehend the fullness of His ways or thoughts. We may even try to grasp some of His logic, but God's logic cannot be understood on the human plane. This is one of the reasons our relationship with God is not based solely on logic, but on trust, faith, and awareness of His Spirit as He reveals His desire for us to move on without understanding the full outcome.

Solomon realized this when he wrote in Proverbs 3:5-6, "Trust in the Lord with all your heart and lean not on your own understanding; in all your ways submit to him, and he will make your paths straight." Paul had a similar mindset when he was talking to the church in Rome:

> Therefore, I urge you, brothers and sisters, in view of God's mercy, to offer your bodies as a living sacrifice, holy and pleasing to God—this is your true and proper worship. Do not conform to the pattern of this world, but be transformed by the renewing of your mind. Then you will be able to test and approve what God's will is—his good, pleasing and perfect will (Romans 12:1-2).

These treasures of Scripture can lead us to a revelation of how to live an entirely dependent life, even in the most uncomfortable or incomprehensible circumstances. It happens, first of all, when we are willing to see the hand, voice, and actions of God, not based on our own understanding, but coming to Him as a living sacrifice, spiritually worshipping God so that we might know His perfect, pleasing, and HOLY will. Do you hear what Paul and Solomon are saying to us? If we take on the mind of Christ and seek God's logic through a heart of faith, trust, and total devotion, we will have a transformed life that will help us even as we endure difficult times when we need His understanding the most. Only when we surrender and become totally dependent on Him will we get to see the perfect, pleasing, and holy will of God.

Not only can we see God's will unfolding, but we get to be a part of it as well. That is more extraordinary than I can even fathom because I keep trying to see it through the eyes of mankind and not through the eyes, expressions, and promises of God. We can connect with God whether we fully grasp Him and His fullness or not. Many people know Him and walk with Him without really understanding what it means to lean on Him.

Throughout the Scripture, God's promises are constantly being shared with us. There are books written around one promise after another. Each day we can read and re-read these books, coming to the realization that the power and difference of God's promise versus man's is that God's promises always have and always will come true. But the paradox of life is that we cannot see or understand those promises when we are living independent lives that are more interested in being comfortable than in being dependent on Him.

The promises of God are created to lead us to dependence on Him, whether it is comfortable or not at the moment, more than to bring us to an understanding. It is a place where we can experience more than the full knowledge of what is going on; it is a place where God resides and wants to meet us as He shows us those promises. He then allows us to choose to step out in faith, even in times of unbelief, and experience a God who will never leave us nor forsake us.

When we are more driven by logic than by faith, we are unable to experience those promises. Don't let my words fool you. I love debating the Scriptures and articulating my faith with the best of them, defending the Gospel as if it needs to be protected by me. We see this in the people of Israel time and again along their journey to the Promised Land. We see it throughout the writings of the prophets when we hear of the disobedience of God's people because they were following the ways of other gods and people instead of Him. We see it in the New Testament when the teachers of the Law continued to chastise and drill Jesus with questions, only to walk away in disbelief. We even see it with the story of Nicodemus in John chapter three, where he sneaked into the place Jesus was staying and in the middle of the night and asked Him, "How does one obtain eternal life?" We read that Jesus gave Nicodemus the answer, but he did not understand. It was not because he was not a brilliant man. As a teacher of the Law, Nicodemus was very smart. The problem was that he was assessing eternal life through the mind and not the heart. It is not about living eternally as much as having an intimate relationship with the Lord, by being dependent, and being, as Jesus said, "born again." These things cannot be proved logically, so we must simply have faith and lean on His promises.

Many people today try to prove to others that the Scripture is God-breathed, and even more try to defend the Bible as simply a good book of wisdom and anecdotes for life that will make us better people. The latter hold that the Bible was written solely by man. How can you prove the reliability of the Word? How can you prove God breathed on the men who wrote it? How can you defend the historicity of the resurrection without accepting the authority of the Bible? We find ourselves in a dilemma if we come to the work and hands of God through the eyes of logic. It is not until we see them through the eyes of faith and lean on those promises that we can see and experience the mystery and wonderful awareness of God incarnate.

I was on an airplane as I wrote part of this chapter. I was busy getting some final thoughts together when the flight attendant asked everyone to shut down their devices. As I was shutting down my computer and reflecting on what I had just written about leaning on the promises of God, I heard a man to my left, one row back, whistling. He was whistling the stanzas and chorus to the song, "Standing on the Promises of God." Was that a coincidence? I do not believe in coincidences. That was God's reassurance to me to keep writing and believing in what I am writing. I should not be amazed by now, but the more I engage in a place of dependence the more I see and experience this kind of phenomena.

"Standing on the Promises" by R. K. Carter

Standing on the promises of Christ my King,
Through eternal ages let His praises ring,
Glory in the highest; I will shout and sing,
Standing on the promises of God.

Refrain:
Standing, standing,

Standing on the promises of God my Savior;
Standing, standing,
I'm standing on the promises of God.

Standing on the promises that cannot fail,
When the howling storms of doubt and fear assail,
By the living Word of God I shall prevail,
Standing on the promises of God.

Standing on the promises I now can see
Perfect, present cleansing in the blood for me;
Standing in the liberty where Christ makes free,
Standing on the promises of God.

Standing on the promises of Christ the Lord,
Bound to Him eternally by love's strong cord,
Overcoming daily with the Spirit's sword,
Standing on the promises of God.

Standing on the promises I cannot fall,
List'ning every moment to the Spirit's call,
Resting in my Savior as my all in all,
Standing on the promises of God.

One of God's promises found in Isaiah 55:11 is that His Word will not return void. What does that mean to you? To me, it means that we get to enter each day worshipping Him as living sacrifices, trusting and believing in what He is doing, and then watch it come back to us again and again. That is His Word and promise. God wants us to experience a progressively deeper relationship with Him, but we continue to pursue our lives the way we want, trying to define ourselves, to make a mark, to seek the impossible dream, and to redefine ourselves. All of that can be good, but if we are doing it in an effort to live life independently instead of dependently on God, then we are moving toward humanism and becoming our own gods, serving our own destiny.

Four Pillars of Leaning on God

Leaning on His promises can look different to each of us. Through my own discovery of the Scriptures and seeing how this act of leaning has played out in my life, I see it as four pillars. These pillars are the very essence of what is necessary in my Christian walk to make this leaning process possible on an ongoing basis. I believe that God has revealed these pillars to me so that I may use them as support and live completely dependent on Him. This is the first and foremost need in my life, but these same pillars can help human relationships grow and become more intimate as well.

The **first** of these pillars is a that of delight. If we want to become more dependent on God, we have to come to a place of delighting in His presence. We can choose to want Him to the point of desiring that kind of relationship. Without this delight, we create an intellectual argument about knowing God without really knowing the essence of *who* He is and how our dependence on Him can flourish to a rich and fulfilling life of abundance with Him. In Psalm 37:1-6 King David says:

> Do not fret because of those who are evil or be envious of those who do wrong; for like the grass they will soon wither, like green plants they will soon die away. Trust in the LORD and do good; dwell in the land and enjoy safe pasture. Take delight in the LORD, and he will give you the desires of your heart. Commit your way to the LORD; trust in him and he will do this: He will make your righteous reward shine like the dawn your vindication like the noonday sun.

David gives us a perfect place of being and what it really means to lean on God. We all have desires and dreams that we seek, and at times we go off on our own journeys, bringing God with us, striving to accomplish those things in hopes that God will give us our desires. We believe that these things, with God's help, will make us comfortable or fulfilled. When we as believers walk with this mindset in our relationship with God and begin to live out the manifestation of our thought processes, why are we confused when we get stuck? It is easy to turn to God and ask for help or direction, but when we do it with this mindset we end up taking control and frequently find ourselves at a dead end.

David gives us a different picture in this passage from the book of Psalms. I would say that this concept of delight causes most men to feel uneasy or uncomfortable and, at times, even anguished. To delight in the Lord is to seek our pleasure in Him and only Him—to embrace life seeking His desires and His passions for us as we find delight in Him. When we do this, God reveals His true desires for our lives.

The problem with us is that we first place the desires in our minds, then we think about ways that God can accomplish them for us. This is not what the passage says. It instructs us to "delight in the Lord," and then those desires within our heart come rolling in. It comes back to the question, "Is God enough?" If everything was stripped away and life as we know it was gone, is He enough? The moment we can truly say that He is enough is when we find our delight in Him, then He actually places those desires and longings in our heart and fulfills them. That means we keep dreaming, learning, growing, and experiencing life, but it is always done in the context of finding our delight in Him.

The **second** pillar is one of desire, of wanting and waiting on Him. Out of delight grows a deeper and deeper desire of wanting more of Him and waiting for Him to reveal Himself. People tend to want God solely for the purpose of giving them what they want. At times we are willing to wait, but only until our patience wears thin or we agree with the direction He is taking us. To desire God is to simply want Him, not for what He can do, but to desire Him and glorify Him in all that we do. When we are in the mode of independence we tend to want God solely because we believe He can heal us, restore our marriages, take care of our finances, or bring us a spouse. That is not desiring Him. That is wanting His ability to do for us so we can have the life we want the way we want it.

Have you ever had a relationship in which you thought someone genuinely liked you, only to discover that it was not you they liked, but what you could do for them or give them at the time? As soon as you are either unable or unwilling to continue giving them what they want, they move on to a new relationship. When that happens you find yourself hurt or bitter because you really thought they wanted you. How often do we put the Lord in that kind of relationship? Dependence is not about what He can do for us, it is about desiring Him so much that we completely get lost in Him, and that what He does is simply a part of who He is. This can only be found when we desire Him more than anything else.

The **third** pillar is the pillar of trust. Let's go back to David's Psalm, "Trust in the Lord and do good" (Psalm 37:3b). In that word "trust" we discover the understanding of unconditional surrender. We are not worried about the outcome because we are trusting that He has complete control of our lives, which includes all outcomes.

Just saying that causes some people to cringe. Can you imagine not knowing your outcome? Can you imagine not feeling in control of a situation, including your desires? To some of us who plan the work and work the plan, it is one of the scariest experiences we can have. Don't we need to feel some control? Not if we trust the Lord God Himself Who knows more, sees more, and truly has our best interest at heart. To trust in the Lord is to keep our eyes on the vertical plane as we move through life knowing that others around us are seeing Him in and through all that we do.

The **fourth** and final pillar is the pillar of faith. In Hebrews 11:1, the author defines faith as: "Now faith is confidence in what we hope for and assurance about what we do not see." Too often we want proof before we step out in faith, but that is an oxymoronic statement if ever I've heard one. Our desire for control is so strong that we want to know the outcome and what is expected of us before we take that step of faith. That is not faith, that is vain confidence that we know what is better for us than a God we cannot see or feel. The reality is that we can't see Him or feel Him until we have faith. Faith is the ability to step out and see what just happened. We live in a delusion if we think we can step out in faith and see what we are stepping into at the same time.

Faith is an intrinsic investment in the unknown. When we step out in faith we receive the gifts of wisdom and knowledge. That is when we discover the God Who created the heavens and the earth. Faith comes out of a heart that says I desire Him, I want to delight in Him, and I want to trust Him. When this happens we truly live in faith and total dependence, finding the relationship that He has longed for us to discover from the beginning of time.

This relationship of leaning allows us to see, feel, and experience those desires—those things that our heart cries out for which move us to a place where we do not need them. They are simply blessings from the Holy One who wants to give us those things as a gift, not as a substitute for Him.

Leaning on these pillars is like a professional football player who weighs 320 pounds, stands six feet three inches tall, and cannot get off the field under his own strength because he has just damaged his knee. If you watch football at all you can visualize this image: a big man with his arms around two other men with his weight placed on their shoulders. He is leaning, but they are neither dragging nor carrying him. They are supporting him so he can stand upright; his direction is totally dependent on them as he hobbles off the field. He is still participating, but completely leaning on them. That is what God desires for us: a heart of dependence as we lean on Him until the time comes that we are no longer aware we are leaning on Him, but are abiding in Him. That is when the two of us become one.

Chapter 23
Unadulterated Dependence

"If you remain in me and I in you, you will bear much fruit" (John 15:5b).

When people think of the state of Washington, where I live, they think of the luscious pines, blue sky, or the rain that falls throughout the seasons. When I tell people I live in the desert region, which comprises two-thirds of the state, they seem surprised. It is in this portion of the state where you discover some of the best apples, pears, cherries, and grapes in the world. This desert region, due to the irrigation canals that have been created, contains some of the richest vegetation in the land. It is amazing to think that we can go outside and pull a fresh apple or pear off a tree. There is nothing better than fresh, hand-picked fruit. What a great gift from God.

This is the image I have in my mind every time I read John 15:

> "I am the true vine, and my Father is the gardener. He cuts off every branch in me that bears no fruit, while every branch that does bear fruit he prunes so that it will be even more fruitful. You are already clean because of the word I have spoken to you. Remain in me, as I also remain in you. No branch can bear fruit by itself; it must remain in the vine. Neither can you bear fruit

> unless you remain in me. I am the vine; you are the branches. If you remain in me and I in you, you will bear much fruit; apart from me you can do nothing." (John 15:1-5).

Jesus is describing a relationship based on more than just leaning on Him; He is describing a relationship in which the vine and the branches are one. The fruit grows on the branches because of its relationship with the vine. "Abiding," or "remaining" as some translations use, speaks of a oneness that words cannot describe. It is a relationship that requires complete dependence on the vine in order for the branches to even conceive of bearing fruit that has value and purpose, and reflects the gardener Himself.

The understanding of abiding is the ability, or resolve, for a person to come into a relationship with God. This requires one to choose to surrender his life, purpose, and control into the hands of the vine itself. People say they want this kind of relationship, but I find in my own life that when the situation gets rough and I am not seeing, feeling, or experiencing a sense of what I want, it becomes easier for me to move to the position I described earlier as independently dependent. In other words, we say we are dependent on God, yet at the same time have our hands on the steering wheel trying to get to the place that provides the greatest comfort. It is hard to feel comfortable when it appears that the outcome isn't going to look the way we want or planned. At that moment we find ourselves in that place of independence as we still try to bear fruit. This is real life. We may bear some fruit, but it has no sustaining value that digs deep into the soul and satisfies our cravings

For example, there have been times that I studied, preached, and gave what I thought was a great sermon. A few people even came to me afterward and said so, but in reality I shared more of myself than of the Lord. We can make our words and actions seem authentic until they undergo the Refiner's fire. Then we realize how many of those words and actions were simply counterfeit.

How many people are living counterfeit lives? They look and feel real, but once you put them through the microscope of trials and tribulations, the truth comes out and you discover that they were putting on a show. True believers live in a manner that moves them from leaning to abiding—from holding on for the moment to becoming resolved that no matter what life throws at them, they are absolutely dependent on Him.

John 15 gives us the picture of the branches that bear fruit. People who are true servants living fully dependent lives will be pruned so that they can bear more fruit. Ouch!!! Who wants that kind of lifestyle? Why would anyone choose to be pruned? Why choose to live in discomfort, or not necessarily getting things the way we want them to be? We do this so we can bear more fruit. How much more does God want to give us, but we are unwilling to allow the fullness of the pruning process to take effect?

For our twenty-fifth wedding anniversary, my wife and I went to Hawaii with her parents who were celebrating their fiftieth anniversary and our children. It was a great week. As a remembrance of that special event I went into a store and bought a young bonsai schefflera that was growing in a volcanic rock and sitting in water. As I purchased the plant, I was told that if I wanted to make the trunk hardy and allow the plant to spring forth new life and become bigger and stronger, I would need to cut off every branch during the June solstice every couple years.

The first time I cut off those small but hardy branches and only saw the trunk sticking out of the rock, I thought I had killed the tree. I waited an agonizing period of time before I saw new life and more branches growing on the trunk, giving it new character. It is the pruning that transforms life, and shapes the heart and mind to think differently. God uses pruning to make our lives more fulfilled. It happens every day, though we seem to only feel it during the intense pruning events. It is in the pruning that the underdeveloped gifts and talents of our lives become more apparent as long as we allow them to grow and flourish. It is the paradoxical moment when everything wonderful starts to happen, and we cannot believe it because it comes in times that are the hardest for us to endure.

The reason it's so hard is that we are still holding on to our independence. We want what we want even though God is telling us to trust Him, have faith in Him, and watch what He does in our lives so that we might live more abundantly. God is not a God of punishment, but sometimes it feels that way because we see everything as work or a struggle. When we are not in the place of resolve, we are not truly abiding in Him. We are not in the place of dependence where all that matters is our heart, mind, and our connection with Him.

David describes that place in Psalm 23:4-5, "Even though I walk through the darkest valley, I will fear no evil, for you are with me; your rod and your staff, they comfort me. You prepare a table before me in the presence of my enemies. You anoint my head with oil; my cup overflows." How many people are blessed out of their socks when they are with their enemies? How many of us are in a place of peace and contentment during those darkest times in our lives when most people want to scream, get angry, or get even? David's cup overflowed. How can that be? It is because he was perfectly abiding in *Yahweh*. If you read the book of 1 Samuel, you will read that King Saul was aware of David being anointed by the prophet and priest Samuel years before David took the throne. With that awareness Saul repeatedly tried to kill David. Over and over again Saul was trying to live as an independent man who sought comfort and guidance from his way of thinking and feeling, even though it brought him nothing but grief.

In 1 Samuel 24, we read of a time when Saul was trying to defeat the Philistines while at the same time seeking to kill David. The Scriptures say that Saul went into a cave to find relief in the same cave where David and his men were hiding. While Saul was sitting there, David sneaked up to him and cut off a portion of His robe. He could have killed Saul and taken His rightful place as king. He could have brought back the fullness of God-filled power. David chose instead not to attack, as shown starting with verse 5:

> Afterward, David was conscience-stricken for having cut off a corner of his robe. He said to his men, "The LORD forbid that I should do such a thing to my master, the LORD's anointed, or lay my hand on him; for he is the anointed of the LORD." With these words David sharply rebuked his men and did not allow them to attack Saul. And Saul left the cave and went his way (1 Samuel 24:5-7).

God prepared for him a table, so to speak, a place where he was with his enemy, and his cup was overflowing with God's presence and power. That is outright dependence. He knew he was to be king, and he knew that someday his hopes and wishes would come true and that God was willing to give him the desires of his heart. All he had to do was keep the Lord as his shepherd and trust in God with all his heart, soul, and mind, and then delight in His ways, His wants, His desires, and his cup overflowed.

Abiding is not easy if we are set in our ways—wanting what we want, when we want, and how we want it—as we continue to seek a balanced life. Life is difficult when we keep getting pruned so that we can see more, give more, share more, and glorify Him in the process. When we truly lean on His will, His way, and His time, we will find peace and joy as our cups overflow. To most people this seems like a paradox, but that is because God is the Great Paradox. We can choose to surrender fully to Him and become one with Him. When we do, He becomes one with us as we begin living that abundant life in His rhythm, stepping onto a huge stone of unadulterated dependence.

Conclusion

I believe that one of the greatest desires that lies within each person is the pursuit of living an abundant life. This may look different to each of us, but that pursuit is there. We have explored in this book what an abundant life in Christ looks like. I have taken you on my own journey of how I came to this message, which I am continuously working to live out through His Spirit.

When I think about this life of abundance, my mind goes to the hit song from ***Man of La Mancha*** entitled "The Impossible Dream." The lyrics are captivating as there is a quest and vitality of life in this song as it speaks of one man's dream, hope, and desire which is in each of us. It may not be so eloquently worded and lived out, but it is there nonetheless. This song describes abundant living.

Imagine a movement of time, space, and human possibilities that can travel either clockwise or counterclockwise. We begin our journey of God's rhythm embracing the heart of the desire of God who says to us I seek a relationship with you. That place is like a stone on the ground that we pick up on our journey as it reminds us where we have been and possibly with whom. It is holding this stone in our hand that we can come to know that God is striving to build a relationship with us. This moment is not about putting Him into our mold or box, or even denying His existence it can be simply about seeing what it is that God desires. As we grow in knowing Him, we encounter another stone where we can reflect on a theological understanding from His perspective, or we choose to seek our own ideological interpretation of Him. With His perspective, we discover yet another stone where we can recall a place or a feeling of discomfort created by our relationship with God that is unfamiliar to our way of thinking and feeling because we have given Him total control. Or we can create a life of comfort that makes sense to us because we are in control.

Finally, we can come to another crossroad and pick up a huge stone. Here we are reminded of an unadulterated dependence that comes from the place of discomfort, where we seek more of Him and His way. The other choice is to continue a life of independence in which we strive to maintain control, seeking things our way, incorporating the use of God language to mask just how independent we want to be. Then we come back to the essence of our journey, which is the relationship itself. That relationship begins and ends the process. We can walk with Him, to His rhythm, or we can pull away and struggle in our independent comfort.

This rhythm beats like a song on earth for those of us who are willing to embrace Him, not just His Word. It is a willingness to be the people He truly desires us to be and do the right things not simply because that is what the Bible says. It is a place where the only assurance we have is in His promises of Himself through His Word, so that we can take His yoke and walk through life seeing through His eyes, with His heart and His mind.

We are so blessed because we are enriched by His beingness in us when we surrender and invite Him into our lives not only as Savior, but as Lord and ruler of the heavens, the earth, and of our lives. The opposite of this peaceful existence in turbulent times is the pursuit of independence, striving for comfort at every turn and creating an ideology that promotes a counterfeit lifestyle of abundance.

We can now see that the rhythm is basically our traveling through life and time clockwise, growing deeper and deeper with Him each time we travel around life, or we stop the process and travel counterclockwise toward a place where our independence and comfort create an ideology that serves our lifestyle, which takes us away from His presence. I have chosen to follow His rhythm as He draws me progressively deeper into seeing His way, His life, and His abundance. There are times in my journey that I slip and begin going counterclockwise, then I stop, grasp that teachable moment, and rejoin the dance. What choices are you making?

I often hear people say that life is not about the destination, but the journey. This is true when we begin our relationship with the Almighty. A relationship with God is a journey in which we get to learn and grow in Him and be a part of what He is doing the way He wants to see it accomplished. We can either live with Him, for Him, and see what He has in store as He fills our hearts, minds, and souls with His Holy presence each day, or we can fight that relationship even as believers, only to move further away from Him. He never changes, He doesn't hide, and He never leaves us nor forsakes us. We are the ones who move to and fro depending on the situations we face, the desires we have, and how much we want to be in control.

The tools to help people share their interpretations are available, but until we are at His mercy and see things the way He wants to show us, we find ourselves living life more *out* of His rhythm than *in* it. Life can be lived abundantly when we are willing to seek first His kingdom and experience things His way. After all, Jesus said in John 14:6, "I am the way and the truth and the life." That life can feel uncomfortable in the beginning, but the more we lean and abide in Him the more we see, live, and feel His abundance, not because of what we are doing, but because of what He is doing in us.

Ephesians 2:10 tells us that we are His workmanship created in Christ Jesus. Let's let Him be the One who takes over so that we can experience the abundant rhythm He created, which begins and ends with Him. I leave you with this prayer that you can use to move to a place of true beingness in His rhythm.

Prayer

Father, I come to you this day aware of Your presence, Your power, and Your longing to love me. I seek to embrace You this day and call upon Your Spirit to guide my heart, thoughts, and actions. Lord, there have been times when I have chosen to take the wheel and see things the way I want to see them, live the way that gives me the greatest comfort for the moment, and live independently as I think, feel, and live as I want to live. I have even been justifying my actions through Your Word simply because I found a verse that promotes that lifestyle. Lord, forgive me. I want to live in Your rhythm; I want to see things through Your eyes, to have Your heart and mind even in the most difficult times in my life. So Lord, I surrender my life to You and I want You as both Lord and Savior, as I get to walk in Your abundance every day seeking Your will and not my own. This I pray in the mighty name of Christ my Lord. Amen!

About the Author

FRANK MAYCOCK is a certified personal and executive coach and founder/owner of Kinetos Coaching. His love and passion in life has been to help people discover the greatness within themselves and the ability to see the power of God. He has been married to his lovely wife Cindy for over 30 years and has two children, a daughter-in-law, and a grandson.

Born in Los Angeles, Dr. Maycock did his undergraduate work in 1973 at Biola University. In 1986, he completed a Master's of Divinity from Fuller Theological Seminary in Pasadena, California with a concentration in marriage and family ministries. In 2006, he earned his Doctorate of Ministry degree from Columbia Theological Seminary with a concentration in Christian Spirituality.

Since the age of nine, Frank has been a believer in Christ. When he was 16, he began to serve Him in many capacities—as a youth pastor, then as an ordained pastor for over 25 years, serving three churches. He then spent five years working at a mission providing food for the needy within his community. In recent years, Frank has ventured into the business sector and now operates a coaching practice.

Dr. Maycock has discovered life can be abundant on Earth as it is in heaven. Abundance doesn't come in the things he has done or does, but in learning to be connected into the Lord's rhythm. He has explored, experienced, and now writes about not living for what he wants, when he wants it, but a life of just being in His presence to be used as God sees fit.

Appendix

A Closer Look at the Rhythm Model

When I started thinking about how I believe God desires us to walk more in terms of rhythm than balance, my mind went to a spiral effect. Each time it goes around it gets closer to the middle, which is where we find that deep relationship with God. The relationship we were created to desire often gets blocked by what we want, when we want, and the way we want, whether it's things, people, or situations.

With that in mind, I started thinking about how to depict God and our relationship with Him I saw an image of the infinity symbol as the most fitting representation of all that God was, is, and will be.

To me, this image represents the sameness of God in terms of time, space, and beingness. As mentioned in Chapter 10, in Exodus 3:13-14 God speaks with Moses about leading the Israelites and Moses asks, "Who do I say sent me?" God replies, "Tell them I AM sent you." In the Hebrew language this is translated "YWH," which we pronounce "*Yahweh*." This is God saying to us, "I am who I am." As I said in the book, it is God who defines Himself. In Hebrews 13:8 the writer of Hebrews tells us, "Jesus Christ is the same yesterday, today, and forever." To me, this speaks of God's consistent nature, never changing, always the same from the beginning of time through eternity. Even though infinity is a mere symbol that does not depict the fullness and splendor of God, for the sake of my understanding I use this construct because it depicts God's rhythm as the same yesterday, today, and forever. He is forever consistent.

The second part of the construct is a spiral that represents our ability to travel through time, space, and around the movements of God each moment, over and over again. This spiral starts at the top and continues to move around and around. It represents us either moving toward God's rhythm in a clockwise direction or away from it in a counterclockwise motion.

We are moving either closer to a deeper relationship with the Lord (clockwise) or further away (counterclockwise). We cannot stay in one place. Time and events tend to heavily influence our choices in that movement for us as we either engage God the way He desires or pull away from Him in pursuit of our own wants. As I see the rhythm unfold before me it appears to be in four seasons.

The **first season** is known as having a **relationship with the Lord**. God always has a relationship with us. We either strive to understand it, choose to believe that God does not exist, or create God in our own image. The first acknowledgement moves us into a relationship with God; the latter two move us into the place of being our own god.

For those who pursue a relationship with God, we move into that **second season** of either **seeing God as He chooses to define Himself** (true theology), which continues to move us in a clockwise direction, or defining God in our own image (ideology), which moves us in a counterclockwise direction that takes us out of the relationship that He desires us to have with us.

The **third season** is the time we move into **discomfort** because the knowledge of God as He chooses to reveal Himself and the space of time we are dealing with makes us uncomfortable. We are uncomfortable because what God is asking of us or revealing to us is a transformation out of our comfort zone into a revelation of how we need to yield our lives to Him. If we choose to stay in our comfort zone, we move counterclockwise, trying to explain away what it is that God is revealing. During these times we begin to rationalize our ideological constructs of why life needs to be the way we want it to be. If we are not careful, we even begin to use what we call theology to move us out of the beingness that God has intended, simply because what we feel, see, and experience makes us comfortable, putting us into a counterclockwise pattern. Remember that the comfort I'm referring to is complacency, that false sense of peace—not rocking the boat or making waves.

The **final season** is one of **dependence or independence**. It is during this season that we either learn to depend on the Lord more and more in our state of discomfort or seek independence, which takes us into a counterclockwise pattern and back to a state of comfort, away from Him. With this thought comes the awareness of our need and desire to be totally dependent on Him to move us deeper and deeper in the life that He desires for us to live.

As we go through these seasons we begin to understand and move with the Lord as He calls us to a deeper place than we have ever been with Him before. Each time we see God, hear His voice, sense His presence, or follow His direction through His Word and the Spirit, we find ourselves moving through these seasons over and over again. As we do, we discover what it is like to be truly one with Him, which is the picture that Jesus describes in John chapters 14 through 17.

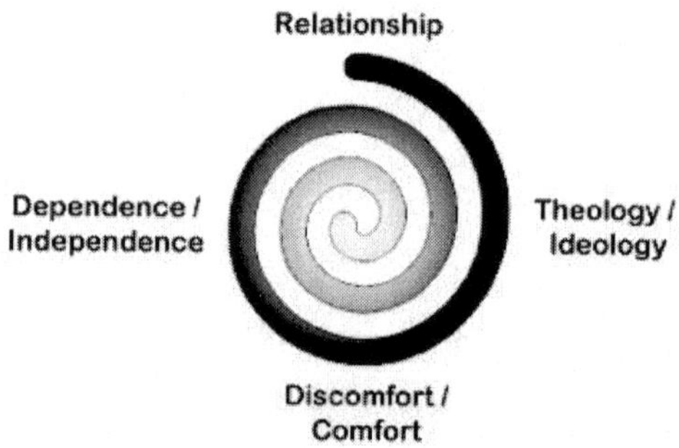

The final diagram looks like this:

In conclusion, we discover that as we move through space and time we can either move closer to God (clockwise) or further from Him (counterclockwise). We can move back and forth, but we are always moving. Through Christ and the Holy Spirit, we can get as close to God as we choose. He has hopes and desires for us, providing we are willing to seek Him and His ways rather than moving away from Him and what He wants from us. This journey, while on earth, is filled with mystery, wonder, and awe, and a yearning within each of us to discover Him as He has manifested His being in us through His Word. We decide whether we want to enter His rhythm, His way, as He chooses us to live it out, or our way seeking what we want, when we want, the way we want it. Do you choose to experience Him by embracing HIS rhythm or do you choose to create your own rhythm? He longs for us to be open to Him as He showers His grace and love upon us in a rich and wholesome way. While on this journey we get to bathe in His grace and mercy and rely on Him while we live and dwell in His beingness as He lives and dwells in ours. This is truly a match made in Heaven.

ORDER YOUR COPY OF FRANK MAYCOCK'S BOOK TODAY

OUT OF BALANCE INTO RHYTHM

FINDING JOY & PEACE AS YOU LIVE LIFE WITH GOD

Are you pursuing the mirage of a balanced life? It's time to stop chasing that illusion and find your rest in God! Forget balance and focus on finding God's rhythm for your life by living His way and not your own. Author Frank Maycock unlocks the secrets to finding the path to living in God's rhythm by going from isolation to relationship, ideology to theology, comfort to discomfort, and independence to dependence. Your rewards for embracing the fullness of His life are accomplishing more than you could ever imagine, knowing more than you thought was possible and finding a God who is more loving and compassionate than you could ever deserve. Begin your journey today.

ISBN: 9781602730786 • 110 pages • $14.95 USD.

"My thoughts are not Your thoughts."
Isaiah 55:8